WHY WE SURVIVE THE WAY WE DO

THE EMOTIONAL LOGIC OF COPING, EXPLAINED THROUGH THE SRTI FRAMEWORK

A. GAETE

HOUSE of TOTO
PRESS

PREFACE

I didn't set out to write a book.

It began in a tattoo chair, somewhere in the middle of a story that I don't even remember.

I've been a quiet student of survival for most of my life, doing the quiet work; reading, journaling, learning how to feel things on purpose. I've gone to therapy, sat in silence, let tattoos hold what I wasn't ready to say out loud, and returned to old wounds with new questions. Healing didn't come all at once. It didn't arrive in clarity. It arrived in fragments. A moment of noticing here, a shift in language there. A gentleness I didn't expect to stay, but did.

Somewhere in that process, this book started to take shape.

I was at Pretty in Ink in Bowie, Maryland—a place that has held more of my healing than it probably knows. I was in the chair, talking without planning to, when someone said something that landed deeper than usual. "You should write a book!" For once, I didn't shut it down.

Something changed that day. Just a little. But it was enough.

I started letting things in, like care, kindness, and company. For someone who had always floated quietly through crisis, it felt disorienting, but it didn't feel wrong.

Letting things in made me realize just how long I'd been keeping everything out.

For years, I thought I was fundamentally broken. I spent two decades searching for the book that would explain me. The one that would make everything inside of me finally make sense. Each book I found seemed to fit for a while, but the relief never lasted. One told me to open up more, another to protect my boundaries; I tried both, and still felt like too much and not enough all at once.

Even in the best parts of my life, the contradictions followed me. I had married the kindest person I know, and we kept circling back to the same arguments; arguments that shouldn't have even existed in the first place. That was when I realized that I wasn't just reacting to the moment. I was reacting to something older, something that never really turned off.

I had shelves full of self-help, psychology, business, management, organization, productivity, and so many memoirs. Each one was a possible answer, none of them was the one that explained me. I kept believing there had to be a book that could. At eleven, my sister-in-law handed me her copy of Dave Pelzer's *A Child Called 'It'*, saying it reminded her of me. That was my first memoir and my introduction to bibliotherapy, though back then I only knew it as the relief of not feeling so alone. While this one book didn't fix anything, it helped me survive, because it showed me that I wasn't alone and that others carried invisible pain too.

As an adult, I continued my search for a book that could do the same thing. I never found it. But over time, something began to take shape. I kept circling the same questions. Something in me needed to make sense of it all, and this is what came out. It started as a journal entry, not a fix, not an answer, just a place to notice the patterns that affected me. Over time, those entries began to turn into a kind of language.

That's what this book is; not a solution, but a language. A way to understand the intelligence in your survival and to see it without judgment.

The frameworks I found helped, but the language often felt clinical, like it belonged to someone else's life. Too often, survival was reduced to symptoms and labels. It didn't sound anything like the life I was living. What I needed was something more human, a way of speaking about survival that didn't turn it into something to fix. That's what this book is meant to offer: another way in.

Wherever you are in your story, you don't have to become someone new.

You're allowed to stay as you are.
This is where healing begins.

FINDING YOUR WAY IN
WELCOME

Survival can be subtle. Sometimes it shows up in ways you barely notice until you look closely. You might overreact to small things or pull away when you want to connect. You feel guilty for resting, needing help, or going numb when things get hard. Maybe you feel like you're watching your own life from a distance.

Staying busy solving, fixing, and caregiving because slowing down feels dangerous. Analyzing your feelings instead of feeling them. There's a reason you freeze up in conflict, work yourself to exhaustion, or feel nothing when something bad happens—because feeling would be too much.

There's nothing wrong with that. You're not broken. You were learning to survive before you even had words for it. Your nervous system—the part of you that scans for safety and threat—did exactly what it was built to do: it kept you safe. But now it's reacting to today like it's still yesterday. It's an echo of a body that never stopped scanning for danger, getting you through childhood, crisis, and chaos exactly the way it was meant to.

Noticing that is the beginning of something new. That's why I built the Survival Response Type Indicator: to name the parts of us that learned to protect, perform, or disappear, and to see why what once kept us safe might now be holding us back.

This book was designed for people who have been living in survival mode. People who might be overwhelmed, exhausted, curious, skeptical, or unsure where to begin. I wrote it with my sister in mind, your typical small-town mom who gives until there's nothing left, who shows up for everyone else but not for herself. I figured if she could see herself here, others might too.

You don't need to read it cover to cover to find something meaningful. You can pause, skip, return, or reread. Whatever your pace, it's the right one.

- Where you begin depends on what you need most: if you're looking for a place to start, you might begin with the self-assessment in Chapter 3. Then read the Survival Type profiles in Chapter 4 to discover your instinctive patterns—how you protect, disconnect, express, and regulate when things feel unsafe. Once you've found your type, come back to Chapters 1 and 2 to explore how these patterns formed and why they once made perfect sense.

- If you already have a sense of your patterns, you may want to skip ahead to the tools, Chapters 7 through 10 focus on growth. You'll explore how your type responds in relationships, daily life, and creative expression. And learn how to gently interrupt old patterns without erasing the intelligence behind them.

- If all of this feels overwhelming, you don't have to take it all in at once: just read the Introduction and Chapter 1. Then pause. There's no pressure to continue right away. Even noticing your patterns is a powerful first step.

The first chapters introduce survival patterns and emotional logic. The middle of the book revisits the four axes, introduces the Survival Archetypes, and begins the shift from awareness into actionable healing. The final chapters bring your type into daily life—relationships, work, friendships, and creativity. And close with an invitation to decide which parts of survival you want to keep, which you're ready to set down, and how to move forward without losing yourself.

However your survival shows up, you don't have to make sense of it alone. This book offers language, context, and care. It was built to hold you while you begin, whether that beginning is quiet, messy, or slow.

There's no wrong way to be here.
Every version of you is welcome.

CHAPTER 1
PERFORMANCE OF SURVIVAL

The moments that should have been simple were the ones that undid me. A casual conversation. A room full of friends. A celebration. On the surface, everything looks fine, but inside, something is unraveling. I keep smiling, but my chest feels hollow, like the sound can't reach me.

I remember it most clearly at a coworker's baby shower, one I had spent weeks planning. She'd been told she would never have children, and then, in her early forties, she learned she was expecting a baby boy. It should have been nothing but joy. And yet, standing there among the balloons and laughter, I felt myself slipping further away.

I wanted it to be perfect. I'd baked for days, driven hours, and made custom gifts and baskets.

The room was full of light and laughter, the air warm with conversation, and it seemed to hold more joy than it could fit. I kept my voice warm and my hands busy. I knew how to look like I belonged, even when I felt miles away; I'd done it my whole life.

Only this time, I noticed when my chest felt hollow, like sound couldn't reach me. I couldn't name what was wrong, I only knew that under the weight of the smiles and chatter, something in me was folding in on itself.

Guests smiled and thanked me for the desserts, the decorations, and I smiled back, nodding, as the hum of conversation wrapped around me. Until I caught a glare from across the room. A woman I didn't know sat stiff in her chair, watching me like I'd taken something from her, and I wanted to disappear; the praise I hadn't wanted clung to me like static.

That was when I realized that I had been performing "okay" for so long, I forgot what being okay actually felt like.

You may not remember when it started. You were useful, agreeable, the one who kept things from falling apart. Maybe you made people laugh, maybe you made yourself small.

Either way, you learned it was safer to be needed than to be known.

Survival isn't always loud. Sometimes it's quiet compliance. It can appear as perfectionism, chronic helpfulness, or the inability to say no.

It can look like having it all together, like strength, success, or independence. Until it breaks you.

It wasn't strength. It was survival—sharp, practiced, invisible

When I was little, I wore "being strong" like armor. I cracked jokes at the exact right time. I handled other people's crises like it was my job. But it wasn't strength, it was fear dressed up like competence. I was terrified of what might happen if I let the mask slip, even for a second.

I never asked for anything back. At funerals, I didn't cry; I sat in the front row, quietly carrying everyone else's grief as if it belonged to me. I showed up sick, bruised, burned out, and called it resilience. But it wasn't.

It was survival. Sharp, practiced, and invisible. I learned to stay safe by staying useful and invisible in all the ways that mattered.

That's what we're exploring here.

Not trauma as a singular event you can point to, but

survival as a way of being. Not the kind that gets headlines or diagnoses, but the kind that gets you through school, work and family dinners.

The kind you don't question because it looks like capability.

That's the thing about performance. Eventually, it disconnects you from your body, from your needs, and the people who love you. You can build a whole life around survival patterns and still feel like you're disappearing inside it.

Maybe you learned to anticipate everyone's needs, because missing the mood once meant punishment. Or you learned to keep your walls high, because vulnerability never felt safe. You may have learned to disappear, to smooth things over, to never show anger or sadness.

And at the time they formed those responses made sense. Some of them formed in childhood. Others got stronger over time. They're not weaknesses. They're evidence that you did what you had to do.

But now? Now you get to ask, *Are they still serving me?*

This is the beginning of noticing and of undoing the performance of survival.

What once kept you safe also kept you unseen.
Now you get to decide if you still carry it.

CHAPTER 2
SURVIVAL MODE

S urvival doesn't always announce itself. Sometimes it's the way you read the room before you've even taken off your coat. The way you measure your words so they land softly. The way you nod along, not because you agree, but because it's easier than explaining. You make sure the chairs are set up, the message is worded just right, and the deadline is met before anyone has a chance to ask.

Other times, it's in the way you fill the silence with a joke. Or keep your face calm when the conversation gets too close. Maybe you say you're fine because the truth feels like is would be too much for the room to hold and you don't want to be a burden.

You don't have to be falling apart to be in survival mode. Sometimes being in survival mode it looks like having it all together. Maybe it looks like capability, reliability, or strength. Whatever it looks like, it can carry a cost.

Over time, you learn to read the room long before you check in with yourself. The line between being responsible and being replaceable begins to blur. And somewhere in the performance of having it all together, you forget what it feels like to belong to yourself.

Somewhere along the way; through families, workplaces, and whole cultures, we learned to measure strength by how much we carry. But survival isn't strength, it's adaptation. It's what happens when something in us decides, I will do whatever I have to do to make it through this.

That could look like silence, people-pleasing, perfectionism, detachment, anger, or control. We develop these strategies early in life to keep us from being hurt, rejected, abandoned, or humiliated, and we repeat them. They keep us alive, but now they can also keep us alone.

The Survival Response Type Indicator uses the Response Pattern Axes (Protector vs. Pleaser, Defender vs. Leaver, Revealer vs. Concealer, Sealer vs. Feeler) to help identify the instinctive responses that were shaped by what once kept you safe.

Each axis highlights a different survival instinct. They're not meant to box you in, but to help you notice your default responses especially when stress takes the wheel. Some people lean hard to one side. Others shift depending on context, relationships, or emotion.

Response Patterns are the instinctive patterns that shape how you survive, relate, and adapt. These aren't fixed personality traits. They're flexible (sometimes even contradictory) responses, that are guided by your nervous system's deep instinct to protect you.

There's no "better" side of this framework, only recognition of the patterns that once protected you.

The more you recognize how you instinctively protect yourself, the more space you create to choose differently.

Let's walk through each axis together.

AXIS 1

Protector (P) ⟵⟶ Pleaser (E)
SOCIAL STRATEGY

Protector (P):

- Responds to a threat by pushing back or guarding.
- Leads with strength, control, or correction.
- May appear intense, reactive, or confrontational.
- Tries to restore order by asserting boundaries or taking charge.

FEELS LIKE: "If I don't act, it will fall apart."
BELIEVES: Safety comes from holding the line.
STRESS RESPONSE: Anger, urgency, control.

Pleaser (E):

- Responds to threat by softening, adapting, or caretaking.
- Tries to preserve peace or connection.
- May appear agreeable, overly flexible, or avoidant.
- Tries to reduce harm by being needed, liked, or non-threatening.

FEELS LIKE: "If I upset them, I'll be rejected."
BELIEVES: Being good, kind, or useful is safe.
STRESS RESPONSE: Anxiety, guilt, over-accommodation.

AXIS 2

Defender (D) ⟷ Leaver (L)
Threat Response

Defender (D):

- Stays put and doubles down under pressure .
- Fights for loyalty, routine, or what's "right".

- Avoids change by reinforcing control or commitment.

FEELS LIKE: "If I walk away, I'm a failure."
BELIEVES: I must prove I'm worthy—or right.
STRESS RESPONSE: Rigidity, overcommitment, loyalty at cost of self.

Leaver (L):

- Escapes or shuts down when overwhelmed.
- Withdraws to regain internal control.
- May leave mentally, emotionally, or physically.

FEELS LIKE: "If I stay, I'll disappear."
BELIEVES: Survival means not being trapped.
STRESS RESPONSE: Disconnection, detachment, emotional retreat.

AXIS 3

Revealer (R) ⟵⟶ Concealer (C)
EMOTIONAL EXPRESSION

Revealer (R):

- Expresses openly, often to seek resonance relief, or understanding
- Shares thoughts, wounds, or insights with ease
- May feel overexposed, misunderstood, or too much

FEELS LIKE: "If I don't say it, I'll feel alone."
BELIEVES: Connection comes from being seen
STRESS RESPONSE: Oversharing, emotional intensity, identity tied to visibility.

Concealer (C):

- Keeps inner world private or compartmentalized
- Shares selectively or not at all
- May appear calm, mysterious, or unreachable

FEELS LIKE: "If I reveal too much, I won't be safe."
BELIEVES: Connection must be earned.
STRESS RESPONSE: Silence, withholding, internal spiraling.

AXIS 4

Sealer (S) ←—→ Feeler (F)
EMOTIONAL REGULATION

Sealer (S):

- Contains or delays emotional responses to maintain control
- Often intellectualizes or minimizes pain
- Appears calm, composed, or emotionally distant

FEELS LIKE: "If I feel too much, I'll fall apart."
BELIEVES: Emotions are messy or dangerous.
STRESS RESPONSE: Numbness, distraction, stoicism.

Feeler (F):

- Experiences emotions vividly, sometimes overwhelmingly.
- Reacts with visible sensitivity, even if hidden later.
- May absorb or mirror others' feelings.

FEELS LIKE: "I don't know how to stop feeling."
BELIEVES: Feeling deeply is necessary, even if it hurts.

Stress response: Emotional flooding, exhaustion, reactivity.

You're not here to fit into a box or be defined by a four-letter code. You're here to notice how you survived—and to honor the ways you kept showing up, even when staying felt impossible.

The real work is this:

- Noticing when your pattern kicks in.
- Naming it with honesty and compassion.
- Choosing something different.

You won't always catch it. You won't always get it right. But every time you notice, something shifts. Every pause holds the potential to shift something. Every quiet recognition is a new direction.

Every moment you notice is a break in the cycle. Your growth is yours alone, and how you express it will be shaped by every part of your story, not just the responses you once needed to survive.

So take what resonates and question what doesn't. And remember: healing isn't becoming someone new—it's returning to who you were before safety had rules.

If something in you has been stirring while you read, maybe small recognitions, or quiet flashes of memory, patterns you can finally name, then you've already begun.

The next step isn't about judgment or fixing. It's about learning the language of your own survival, so you can hear what it's been saying all along.

It wasn't weakness.
It was survival, and it makes sense.

CHAPTER 3
SELF-ASSESSMENT
SURVIVAL RESPONSE TYPE INDICATOR

The Survival Response Type Indicator is a self-reflection framework that maps the patterns of your survival instincts across four core axes. Each axis captures one dimension of how you instinctively respond to threat, stress, or vulnerability. Together, the four axes create a type code that reflects your nervous system's familiar patterns —not as a label, but as a lens you can use to understand yourself more clearly.

You've already started to map the shape of your survival— the moments that formed it, the logic that held it together, the ways it kept you safe. You may notice pieces of yourself clicking into place, parts of your story that finally make sense. These aren't just fragments of the past. They're the foundation for what comes next.

The self-assessment you're about to take isn't here to label or limit you. It's here to reflect back patterns you may have internalized without realizing. Like any mirror, it won't capture everything—but it will give you a starting point. A way to name what your nervous system learned to do when it was trying to keep you safe.

Some questions may feel familiar. Others may stir discomfort. All of that is part of the process. You don't need to over-think your answers. Trust your first instinct. Trust that you know more about your survival than you've ever been given credit for.

This is not a test. There are no wrong answers. There is only the quiet intelligence of how you adapted—and the beginning of learning what to do with that knowledge now.

~

This self-assessment invites you to notice how you instinctively respond when things feel uneasy. There are four axes, each looking at a different way you protect, stay, feel and connect. You'll answer **40 multiple-choice questions**, ten per axis. For each, choose the response that feels most natural or true—even if you wish it weren't.

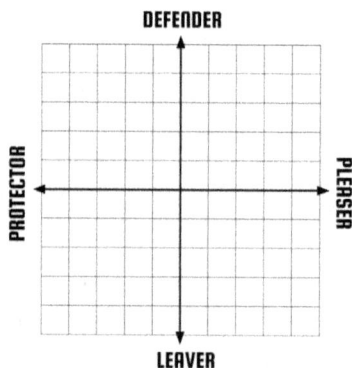

After each axis, you'll answer ten questions and tally your scores to see which side you lean toward (A/B). If it's close, there's a tie-breaker reflection to guide your final call.

Axis 1: Protector (P) vs Pleaser (E) - explores how you respond to tension, conflict, or emotional discomfort—especially when something you care about feels at risk.

AXIS 2: DEFENDER (D) vs. LEAVER (L) - explores how you respond when something feels threatening, destabilizing, or painful—especially in relationships or identity.

AXIS 3: REVEALER (R) vs. CONCEALER (C) - explores how you handle emotional visibility.

AXIS 4: SEALER (S) vs. FEELER (F) - explores how your body and nervous system regulate emotion—especially under stress.

Please answer **A or B** for each of the following. There are no right answers—just what feels most like you, especially under stress or emotional strain.

AXIS 1: PROTECTOR (P) VS PLEASER (E)

This section explores how you instinctively respond to relational tension, like whether you tend to hold your ground or soften to keep the peace.

1. **In a tense conversation, I'm more likely to...**
   a. Say what I really think, even if it creates discomfort.
   b. Find a way to keep the peace, even if it means softening or hiding my truth.
2. **When someone crosses my boundary, I tend to...**
   a. Pull back or push back, my walls go up fast.
   b. Question whether I was being too sensitive or unclear.
3. **Growing up, I felt safest when I was...**
   a. In control, strong, or emotionally guarded.
   b. Helpful, agreeable, or emotionally in tune with others.
4. **When someone's upset with me, I usually...**
   a. Feel defensive or shut down.
   b. Feel responsible and want to fix it.
5. **My instinct when someone needs help is to...**
   a. Assess whether they're taking advantage. I'm careful with my energy.
   b. Step in automatically. I don't want to let anyone down.
6. **When I feel emotionally overwhelmed, I...**
   a. Get quiet, angry, or distant.
   b. Get anxious, apologetic, or try to make others comfortable.
7. **I worry more about...**
   a. Being manipulated, controlled, or vulnerable.

     b. Being disliked, a burden, or too much.

8. **In conflict, I tend to...**
   a. Double down, defend, or try to win.
   b. Backtrack, soothe, or look for compromise.

9. **I feel most powerful when I'm...**
   a. Independent, grounded, or standing my ground.
   b. Connected, appreciated, or making others feel better.

10. **After an argument, I'm more likely to...**
    a. Withdraw to protect myself.
    b. Reach out to repair or smooth things over.

*Total your a's and b's for each axis, then record the letter (P/E) into the first place for your type code.

A → Protector (P)

B → Pleaser (E)

If tied: use the below tie-breaker prompt.

When you feel tension in a relationship, do you move toward harmony or toward truth?

Choosing **harmony** → Pleaser (E)

Choosing **truth** → Protector (P)

Write your result letters in order from each axis:
YOUR RESULT FOR AXIS 1: P OR E

YOUR TYPE CODE: __↓__ ____ ____ ____

AXIS 2 - DEFENDER (D) VS. LEAVER (L)

This Axis allows you to reflect on how you cope when stress feels overwhelming: do you stay and fight, or retreat to protect yourself? Trust your first instinct; these questions simply mirror what feels most true for you under pressure.

1. **When I feel misunderstood or attacked, I'm more likely to...**
   a. Explain myself, clarify, or dig in.
   b. Withdraw, shut down, or mentally check out.
2. **If I feel someone is slipping away, I tend to...**
   a. Try harder to stay close or fix what's wrong.
   b. Emotionally distance first to avoid getting hurt.
3. **When I'm triggered, my default response is to...**
   a. Engage. I want to resolve it.
   b. Disengage. I need to escape it.
4. **In group conflict, I'm usually the one who...**
   a. Takes a stand or mediates.
   b. Leaves, ghosts, or zones out.
5. **When something hurts, I often...**
   a. Ruminate or replay it in my head.
   b. Numb out or move on fast.
6. **If someone I care about criticizes me, I usually...**
   a. Feel a need to defend myself or explain.
   b. Feel ashamed and want to disappear.
7. **In conflict, I feel...**
   a. Overly responsible or reactive.
   b. Detached or emotionally absent.
8. **In relationships, I often fear...**
   a. Being too much.
   b. Being forgotten or fading out.

9. **In the past, when someone crossed a boundary...**
   a. I said something, even if awkward.
   b. I silently distanced myself.

10. **I usually notice I'm struggling when...**
   a. My thoughts get loud and looping.
   b. My energy drops, and I feel empty.

*Total your a's and b's for each axis, then record the letter (D/L) into the second place for your type code.

A → Defender (D)

B → Leaver (L)

If tied: use the below tie-breaker prompt.
   When things feel broken or uncertain, do you feel safer staying, even if it's painful, or do you feel safer leaving, even if it hurts?

Choosing **staying** → Defender (D)

Choosing **leaving** → Leaver (L)

Write your result letters in order from each axis:
YOUR RESULT FOR AXIS 2: D OR L

YOUR TYPE CODE: ____ __↓__ ____ ____

AXIS 3 - REVEALER (R) VS. CONCEALER (C)

This section invites you to consider how openly you share your inner world. Notice whether you tend to voice your emotions or keep them contained, and respond with honesty and curiosity, without needing justification or minimizing.

1. **When something upsets me, I'm more likely to...**
   a. Talk about it, even if I downplay it or joke.
   b. Keep it inside, I need to process privately.
2. **I'm often told that I'm...**
   a. Honest, expressive, or "too open" sometimes.
   b. Private, mysterious, or "hard to read".
3. **When someone asks how I'm doing, I usually...**
   a. Answer honestly, even if it's awkward.
   b. Say "I'm fine" even when I'm not.
4. **When I cry or get emotional in front of others, I tend to feel...**
   a. Relieved or more connected.
   b. Exposed, ashamed, or out of control.
5. **I prefer...**
   a. Letting people see my emotions, even messy ones.
   b. Staying composed and in control.
6. **If someone I care about is distant or quiet, I tend to...**
   a. Ask them what's wrong and talk it through.
   b. Wait and hope they'll come around on their own.
7. **In conflict, I usually...**
   a. Say what I feel, even if I get emotional.
   b. Shut down or hold back until I'm alone.
8. **My fear around vulnerability is usually...**
   a. Being too much or too needy.

     b. Being seen as weak or emotional.
9. **In close relationships, I often...**
     a. Overshare or lead with honesty.
     b. Keep parts of myself hidden, even from those I love.
10. **I tend to feel safest when...**
     a. People know what's really going on with me.
     b. I'm in control of what others see.

*Total your a's and b's for each axis, then record the letter (R/L) into the third place for your type code.

A → Revealer (R)

B → Concealer (C)

If tied: use the below tie-breaker prompt.
When you're overwhelmed, does it feel safer to contain it or express it?

Choosing **share it** → Revealer (R)

Choosing **keep it sacred** → Concealer (C)

Write your result letters in order from each axis:
YOUR RESULT FOR AXIS 3: R OR C

YOUR TYPE CODE: ____ ____ __↓__ ____

AXIS 4 - SEALER (S) VS. FEELER (F)

This section asks you to notice how you handle emotional intensity, whether you lean toward containing feelings or experiencing them fully. Choose the response that best reflects your usual pattern; every response is valid.

1. **How do you experience emotions in the moment?**
   a. I usually don't feel my emotions until later, if at all.
   b. I often feel my emotions right away, even when I wish I didn't.
2. **How do you try to manage emotions?**
   a. I try to keep emotions in check and avoid getting swept up.
   b. I feel things deeply, even if I try not to show it.
3. **What happens when you're stressed or triggered?**
   a. I shut down or numb out to stay calm.
   b. My body reacts even when I try to stay calm.
4. **How do you handle emotionally intense situations?**
   a. I can stay in control emotionally.
   b. I sometimes feel ruled by my emotions.
5. **What feedback have you received from others?**
   a. I've been told I'm too cold or distant.
   b. I've been told I'm too sensitive or dramatic.
6. **When overwhelmed, what's your instinctive response?**
   a. I go numb or disconnect.
   b. I feel everything, often all at once.
7. **How do you handle crying?**
   a. I try not to cry, even when I want to.
   b. I cry easily, even when I don't want to.

8. **How do you handle emotions when there's something you need to get done?**
    a. I can set emotion aside and stay focused.
    b. Emotion bleeds into everything; it's hard to separate.
9. **How do you relate to feelings overall?**
    a. I suppress feelings; they feel like a distraction.
    b. I express feelings, and they feel like a release.
10. **Which statement describes your emotional struggle best?**
    a. I struggle more with not feeling enough.
    b. I struggle more with feeling too much.

*Total your a's and b's for each axis, then record the letter (S/F) into the fourth place for your type code.

A → Sealer (S)

B → Feeler (F)

If tied: use the below tie-breaker prompt.
When something is deeply personal, do you feel drawn to share it or keep it secret?

Choosing **secret** → Sealer (S)

Choosing **share** → Feeler (F)

Write your result letters in order from each axis:
YOUR RESULT FOR AXIS 4: S OR F

YOUR TYPE CODE: ____ ____ ____ __↓__

Write your result letters in order from each axis: This four-letter code represents your **current dominant survival pattern**, how you protect, stay, feel, and connect.

Your Type Code:____ ____ ____ ____

CHAPTER 4
SURVIVAL RESPONSE TYPES
YOUR PATTERN, DECODED

Right now, your four letters might look ordinary, just a code you've written down. But they're more than that. They're the quiet map of how you've made it through: the ways you've learned to protect yourself, the places you've stayed, the feelings you've carried, the connections you've kept or let go.

Each letter is a trace of moments when you adjusted, softened, held back, or stood your ground because that was what kept you safe.

Each of us developed these survival patterns to stay safe, connected, or in control. Your four-letter code reflects how your nervous system responds under pressure and what you've carried to survive.

In the pages ahead, we'll walk through what each type means—not as a diagnosis, but as a language. You'll see the patterns your code describes, and maybe, the parts of yourself you've felt but never quite named.

THE STRATEGIST (ELCF)

Pleaser / Leaver / Concealer / Feeler

While they debated, you opened a fresh tab and made a plan. You didn't raise your voice. You didn't need to. Steady felt safer than uncertain, and no one noticed the weight you were managing behind your calm.

Core Instinct

Stay ahead. Stay calm. Stay useful.

Snapshot

Highly analytical and emotionally attuned, Strategists often take on responsibility early. They manage chaos with logic and tend to anticipate needs before others express them. They find safety in control—but underneath, they're driven by care. Many struggle with burnout from over-functioning and a quiet fear of becoming irrelevant.

Axes in Action

E – You appease and adapt, often smoothing tension to maintain emotional safety.

L – You withdraw when overwhelmed, recalibrating in solitude.

C – You manage discomfort through structure and mental clarity.

F – You feel deeply, even when you hide it.

Life Through This Lens

You stay calm under pressure, but carry the weight of everyone else's chaos in silence. People praise your competence but rarely ask how you're really doing.

Where It Began

Often raised in environments where emotional safety was unpredictable, you learned that controlling outcomes could reduce conflict. You were the dependable one—perhaps too early.

How This Shows Up

IN CONFLICT: You avoid emotional messiness, opting for practical solutions.

IN WORK: You excel in crisis and planning.

IN FRIENDSHIP: You feel hurt when others don't see how much you're doing.

IN CREATIVITY: You channel your care into structure and purpose.

IN GROWTH: You must learn that usefulness is not your only value.

Reflection: Who are you without offering?

THE TACTICIAN (ELCS)

Pleaser / Leaver / Concealer / Sealer

You hold it together by staying ahead of the details. The grocery list, the project plan, the calendar alert—if it's accounted for, it can't fall apart. When things feel messy, you tighten the routine. It's not control for the sake of control. It's how you breathe easier.

Core Instinct
Stay useful. Stay composed. Don't get messy.

Snapshot
Practical and measured, Tacticians create order through structure. They're dependable, prepared, and often behind the scenes—making things work without asking for credit. They avoid emotional messiness, preferring action over expression. But under the surface, the effort to stay composed can be isolating. They often internalize failure and quietly wonder if anyone sees how much they're holding.

Axes in Action
E – You try to preserve harmony, even at your own expense.
L – You retreat from emotional overwhelm and regroup privately.
C – You manage situations with logic and efficiency.
S – You suppress emotional turbulence to keep things running smoothly.

Life Through This Lens
You take comfort in structure and clarity. Feelings are data, but not always useful. Control keeps the noise down—but sometimes you wonder what it's costing you to keep it that quiet.

Where It Began
You likely grew up in a space where emotional restraint was

encouraged—or where stability required you to stay small and steady. Being useful became your way of mattering.

How This Shows Up

IN CONFLICT: You go quiet, focus on fixing, and avoid escalation.

IN WORK: You're the backbone—organized, calm, reliable.

IN FRIENDSHIP: You show up through action, not emotional display.

IN CREATIVITY: You prefer tangible, practical forms of expression.

IN GROWTH: You begin naming what you feel before you solve it.

Reflection: What emotions are hiding beneath your to-do list?

THE MEDIATOR (ELRF)

Pleaser / Leaver / Revealer / Feeler

At dinner, when her parents bickered, she'd pass the salt with a smile and change the subject before the heat could build. She wasn't trying to manipulate—it was just instinct to keep things gentle.

Core Instinct
Keep the peace. Keep everyone okay.

Snapshot
Empathic and adaptive, Mediators blend into groups and smooth tension. You read emotional tone intuitively and often prioritize harmony without even realizing it. But in constantly tending to others, you may lose track of where you begin. Over time, it becomes hard to know what you want when no one else is asking.

Axes in Action
E – You prioritize relationships over personal preference.
L – You disengage when situations feel emotionally charged.
R – You adapt to emotional shifts and needs with flexibility.
F – You feel deeply and often absorb the emotions of others.

Life Through This Lens
You want everyone to feel okay. When others are upset, you instinctively scan for how to make it right—before they even ask. But when the room is finally quiet, you're not always sure what you need. You feel connected to everyone, but sometimes wonder if anyone truly sees you.

Where It Began
You likely grew up needing to manage or monitor the emotional tone of your environment. Care may have felt conditional on your ability to maintain calmness.

How This Shows Up

IN CONFLICT: You accommodate or diffuse, then disappear.

IN WORK: You're the team glue, anticipating needs and filling gaps.

IN FRIENDSHIP: You give more than you receive.

IN CREATIVITY: You work best when you feel emotionally safe.

IN GROWTH: You begin asking, "What do *I* want?"

Reflection: What truths would your needs tell if you stopped silencing them?

THE DIPLOMAT (ELRS)

Pleaser / Leaver / Revealer / Sealer

The moment tension rose, you softened your words. You found the middle, even when you didn't agree. That's how you stay safe: not by disappearing completely, but by keeping things from tipping too far.

Core Instinct
Stay neutral. Stay calm. Don't make it worse.

Snapshot
Calm, capable, and composed, Diplomats are peacekeepers who manage situations with poise. They tend to minimize their own needs and often cope by staying neutral. But over time, being the steady one can start to feel like being unseen. You become known for keeping the peace—even when it's costing you yours.

Axes in Action
E – You smooth things over to keep the connection.
L – You emotionally withdraw when overwhelmed.
R – You shift yourself to keep the peace.
S – You seal off emotional intensity to avoid volatility.

Life Through This Lens
You value peace, even if it means silencing your own discomfort. You often believe it's better to say nothing than risk making things worse. But holding it in doesn't mean it doesn't hurt. Over time, quiet becomes a habit—and then a hiding place. You wonder if anyone really knows how much effort it takes to seem unaffected.

Where It Began
You may have been raised in an environment where expressing emotion created instability or backlash. You learned that neutrality was safety.

How This Shows Up

IN CONFLICT: You understate your feelings to de-escalate the situation.

IN WORK: You keep things organized and low-drama.

IN FRIENDSHIP: You're supportive but may feel invisible.

IN CREATIVITY: You prefer clean, composed forms of expression.

IN GROWTH: You reclaim your right to take up space.

> **Reflection**: What truth have you been protecting others from, at your own expense?

THE ADVOCATE (EDCF)

Pleaser / Defender / Concealer / Feeler

You're the one who stays on the phone until 2 a.m., making sure everyone else is okay—even when you're barely holding it together yourself. It's easier to help than to ask for help. Carrying someone else's pain feels more manageable than facing your own.

Core Instinct
Protect others. Hold it together.

Snapshot
Warm and justice-oriented, Advocates feel compelled to protect others. They often take on emotional caretaking roles and step in where others hesitate to do so. They struggle with guilt and overidentifying with other people's pain. Can neglect their own needs in the process.

Axes in Action
E – You respond to distress by helping or fixing.
D – You keep your emotional responses private to hold things together.
C – You try to manage and contain emotional disruption.
F – You feel with intensity and depth.

Life Through This Lens
You lead with your heart, even when it hurts. You carry other people's pain like it's yours to fix—and feel guilty when you can't. However, always being the strong one can be lonely. Sometimes you wonder if anyone really sees you, or just what you do for them.

Where It Began
You likely grew up in a system where someone needed defending, and you stepped in to help. Over time, this became your identity: the one who protects.

How This Shows Up

IN CONFLICT: You mediate or intervene to protect the vulnerable.

IN WORK: You go beyond your role to ensure others feel supported.

IN FRIENDSHIP: You show love through acts of care and advocacy.

IN CREATIVITY: You express meaning through emotionally charged themes.

IN GROWTH: You learn that rescuing isn't the same as connection.

> **Reflection**: What would change if you offered yourself the same compassion you give others?

THE ADVISOR (EDCS)

Pleaser / Defender / Concealer / Sealer

You carried the charger, the allergy meds, and the backup plan. You always think ahead—because someone has to. People call you thoughtful, but they don't see the pressure behind it. That part stays quiet.

Core Instinct

Stay steady. Stay helpful. Don't need too much.

Snapshot

Wise, loyal, and composed, Advisors are quiet stabilizers. They're often the person others go to for help, but rarely ask for it themselves. Over time, that steadiness can start to feel like invisibility. People count on you, but rarely check in.

Axes in Action

E – You aim to be helpful and non-disruptive.
D – You remain consistent even when things get hard.
C – You meet others' needs by offering structure and predictability
S – You contain emotion to prevent instability.

Life Through This Lens

You don't like chaos. You feel best when things are calm and functional, even if that means you're overlooked. But being the dependable one doesn't mean you don't need care. You just learned early that staying quiet was safer than being disappointed.

Where It Began

You were likely praised for being mature, helpful, or low-maintenance. Over time, you learned that needing less meant being valued more.

How This Shows Up

IN CONFLICT: You stay grounded, rarely escalating.

IN WORK: You're dependable and systems-oriented.

IN FRIENDSHIP: You support others but rarely open up.

IN CREATIVITY: You prefer technical, refined expressions of meaning.

IN GROWTH: You begin expressing needs, not just meeting them.

Reflection: What would happen if you let others support you?

THE COMPANION (EDRF)

Pleaser / Defender / Revealer / Feeler

You sense what someone needs before they say a word. You bring soup, send a check-in text, and stay on the phone longer than you should. And afterward—when the room is quiet—you feel the ache you tucked away to show up soft.

Core Instinct
Stay close. Stay soft. Stay useful.

Snapshot
Gentle, loyal, and emotionally responsive, Companions find identity in connection. They offer depth in relationships but may avoid autonomy. Prone to enmeshment or losing themselves in the service of others' needs. Often have deep wells of untapped creativity. Over time, always showing up for others can start to feel like disappearing.

Axes in Action
E – You prioritize relationships and try to avoid conflict.
D – You stay committed even when it's difficult.
R – You adapt to others' needs and rhythms.
F – You feel and respond with emotional sensitivity.

Life Through This Lens
You want closeness more than certainty. You feel deeply and intuitively, often adjusting your shape to stay connected. But when your worth is tied to being needed, it's easy to forget where you end and someone else begins. You wonder if they love you, or just how you make them feel.

Where It Began
You may have grown up feeling that love required attunement and loyalty. You became someone who listened more than asked.

How This Shows Up

IN CONFLICT: You avoid escalation and seek reconnection.

IN WORK: You focus on team harmony and emotional dynamics.

IN FRIENDSHIP: You offer warmth but may struggle to assert needs.

IN CREATIVITY: You express emotion through connection and care.

IN GROWTH: You begin reclaiming your own desires.

> **Reflection**: What do you need when you're not being needed?

THE ANCHOR (EDRS)

Pleaser / Defender / Revealer / Sealer

You sit with her through the panic, breathing slowly so she can borrow your calm. No one asks how you slept that night—you didn't, but that's not what matters. You're used to being the safe place, even when it costs you peace.

Core Instinct
Keep everyone steady—even if I sink.

Snapshot
Grounded and present, Anchors regulate others by simply existing with calm. They tend to avoid extremes and remain emotionally steady. Often under-acknowledged because of how seamlessly they adapt. May silence their truth to maintain peace. The more stable you are for others, the harder it becomes to show when you're not okay.

Axes in Action
E – You respond to tension with care and calm.
D – You remain connected through difficulty.
R – You adapt in the moment to maintain peace.
S – You contain personal emotion to stabilize others.

Life Through This Lens
You feel responsible for maintaining balance. Others turn to you in crisis, but may not notice when you're drowning. You hold their weight without complaint—but it builds. Over time, the silence becomes a burden. You start to wonder if there's any space left for your own storm.

Where It Began
You likely learned early that the best way to stay safe was to stay steady. Expressing need or volatility may have the disrupted connection.

How This Shows Up

IN CONFLICT: You de-escalate and internalize.

IN WORK: You hold teams together with quiet stability.

IN FRIENDSHIP: You're loyal and generous but quietly overextended.

IN CREATIVITY: You channel emotion into grounded, under-stated expression.

IN GROWTH: You learn that being calm doesn't mean being silent.

Reflection: Who helps you stay upright when you're holding everything?

THE PILLAR (PLCF)

Protector / Leaver / Concealer / Feeler

When your best friend was spiraling, you brought tea and sat on the floor beside her. You didn't say much—you didn't have to. That's how you love: steady, quiet, close. But later, you carried the weight alone, like always.

Core Instinct
Keep everyone warm—but don't burn too bright.

Snapshot
Protective and quietly intense, Pillars are emotionally rich under a composed exterior. You stay loyal, attuned, and deeply caring—but only a few get to see that side. You guard your heart with gentleness, not walls, and tend to soothe others while hiding your own vulnerability. Over time, always being present but never fully revealed can leave you feeling invisible in the rooms you never left.

Axes in Action
E – You tend to others with warmth and accommodation.
C – You filter your emotional expression, revealing it selectively.
R – You remain present and connected through discomfort.
F – You feel deeply and can't help but care.

Life Through This Lens
You want to be close, but fear being too much. You know how to stay, even when it's hard, and often take emotional responsibility for the room. But hiding your tenderness eventually starts to ache. You wonder what it would feel like to be held as deeply as you hold.

Where It Began

You likely learned that expressing emotion came with consequences—or wasn't welcomed. So you stayed close, stayed quiet, and kept your tenderness tucked safely inside.

How This Shows Up

In CONFLICT: You de-escalate or quietly withdraw to avoid rejection.

In WORK: You offer consistent support without needing credit.

In FRIENDSHIP: You nurture deeply but may hide how much you're hurting.

In CREATIVITY: You express through careful craftsmanship and soulful nuance.

In GROWTH: You begin to let others witness your depth without shrinking it.

Reflection: What if your tenderness didn't have to hide?

THE COMMANDER (PLCS)

Protector / Leaver / Concealer / Sealer

When things fell apart, you stepped in with a clipboard and a plan. Emotions could wait—someone had to lead. That's how you care: calm voice, clear fix, no mess. Even if it costs you more than anyone realizes.

Core Instinct
Take charge. Shut it down. Keep it moving.

Snapshot
Directive, competent, and strategic, Commanders prefer control to vulnerability. They lead with logic and have little tolerance for inefficiency. Often dismisses emotional needs—both their own and others'. Underneath, they may fear dependence or emotional chaos. No one sees the care that is hidden behind the command, or how lonely it can be to always go first.

Axes in Action
P – You take charge when others hesitate.
L – You detach when overwhelmed or frustrated.
C – You organize, lead, and solve with clarity.
S – You compartmentalize emotion to avoid a mess.

Life Through This Lens
You want order, not chaos. So you avoid the feelings that might rearrange everything. You're more comfortable fixing problems than feeling them. But even leaders long to rest. The more you keep everything together, the harder it becomes to let anyone see when you're falling apart.

Where It Began
You may have grown up in a system where vulnerability was punished, or where emotional needs created disorder. Leadership became your shield.

How This Shows Up

IN CONFLICT: You become blunt, efficient, or dismissive.

IN WORK: You command respect and manage outcomes.

IN FRIENDSHIP: You're protective, but private.

IN CREATIVITY: You prefer mastery and control over vulnerability.

IN GROWTH: You learn that emotions aren't the enemy.

> **Reflection**: What are you afraid might happen if you let someone see your softness?

THE RESCUER (PLRF)

Protector / Leaver / Revealer / Feeler

You pulled over without thinking—heart racing, hands steady—because that's what you do. Help first. Feel later. It's not about being a hero. It's about not knowing how to stay still when someone's hurting.

Core Instinct

Help now. Feel later. Fix it fast.

Snapshot

Driven by empathy and purpose, Rescuers leap into action when others are hurting. They often come from backgrounds where help had to be earned. They tend to overextend and feel responsible for others' outcomes. Prone to emotional exhaustion. Underneath the urgency is a quiet depletion—one they rarely stop long enough to feel.

Axes in Action

P – You move to protect or fix as a first instinct.
L – You withdraw to regroup but return quickly when needed.
R – You adapt to support others in distress.
F – You feel compelled to act on others' suffering.

Life Through This Lens

You carry others' pain in your body. You act fast to ease it—sometimes before understanding your own limits. But when the dust settles, there's no room left for your own ache. You soothe everyone but yourself, unsure how to sit with what you've buried.

Where It Began

You may have been the helper in a home full of unmet needs. You learned to soothe pain not with presence, but with action.

How This Shows Up

IN CONFLICT: You intervene, soothe, or fix—even when exhausted.

IN WORK: You're dependable in crisis, often to your own detriment.

IN FRIENDSHIP: You overextend, then withdraw to recover.

IN CREATIVITY: You express emotion through service or storytelling.

IN GROWTH: You reclaim your energy as your own.

Reflection: What part of you needs rescuing most?

THE WARDEN (PLRS)

Protector / Leaver / Revealer / Sealer

You smiled, you stayed, but you didn't unpack. You never do. It's not fear—it's the safety of knowing you can leave when you need to. That's how you've learned to stay: loosely.

Core Instinct
Stay quiet. Stay safe. Watch everything.

Snapshot
Private and observant, Wardens protect by withholding. They value integrity and show care through action more than words. Deep feelers underneath a cool exterior. May be mistaken for cold when they are actually cautious. Boundaries are sacred.
But the longer you go unseen, the harder it becomes to ask to be known.

Axes in Action
P – You take action when needed, but quietly.
L – You exit emotionally or physically under stress.
R – You adjust your presence to maintain safety.
S – You seal your emotions behind strong internal walls.

Life Through This Lens
You are alert to danger and manage your visibility accordingly. Your quiet is mistaken for distance, but it's really protection.
You crave closeness, but vulnerability feels like a risk you never learned how to take. So you stay behind the walls you built, hoping someone might still see through.

Where It Began

You likely grew up in a place where trust was earned slowly or violated easily. Caution became your compass.

How This Shows Up

IN CONFLICT: You stay composed, sometimes distant.

IN WORK: You prefer autonomy and quiet integrity.

IN FRIENDSHIP: You offer loyalty but guard your inner world.

IN CREATIVITY: You express through precision, metaphor, or privacy.

IN GROWTH: You begin to risk being seen.

> **Reflection**: What part of you longs to be known—even if it's scared?

THE GUARDIAN (PDCF)

Protector / Defender / Concealer / Feeler

You walk on the outside of the sidewalk, instinctively placing yourself between danger and the people you love. No one asks why—but you do it every time. Protection isn't something you talk about. It's just who you are.

Core Instinct
Step in. Hold strong. Keep others safe.

Snapshot
Steady and bold, Guardians act like emotional bodyguards. You carry what others can't. Often it's the one between harm and the people you love. Fiercely loyal, deeply grounded. Leadership often came early and at a cost.
You're strong for everyone, but some days you wonder if anyone sees the weight you never set down.

Axes in Action
P – You respond protectively when others are vulnerable.
D – You stay loyal, even when it's hard.
C – You manage outcomes to prevent chaos.
F – You feel deeply and are driven by empathy.

Life Through This Lens
You feel responsible for others' safety—emotionally, physically, and spiritually. You don't always talk about what you carry. You just carry it.
There's a quiet ache that builds over time, not from the effort itself, but from how rarely anyone offers to hold it with you.

Where It Began
You may have grown up in a role where others leaned on you too soon. Care became identity. Control became survival. You learned that being strong was the only option.

How This Shows Up

IN CONFLICT: You take charge, especially when others freeze.

IN WORK: You anticipate needs and shoulder burdens.

IN FRIENDSHIP: You protect with loyalty and depth.

IN CREATIVITY: You build things that last.

IN GROWTH: You learn to let others hold you.

Reflection: What would happen if you stopped holding it all?

THE DIRECTOR (PDCS)

Protector / Defender / Concealer / Sealer

Your calendar has color codes, backup plans, and margin notes. You can hold a team together without saying much, but no one sees how much you're holding in just to keep things running.

Core Instinct

Stay focused. Stay in control. Don't drop the ball.

Snapshot

Capable and composed, Directors lead quietly and effectively. You hold high standards for yourself and others. Emotion doesn't rattle you, but intimacy might. Love often gets translated into responsibility.

You carry the weight of everything running smoothly, but rarely let on how much you long to be off-duty, even just for a moment.

Axes in Action

P – You protect others by organizing and leading.
D – You stay when things are hard and see them through.
C – You prefer structure, systems, and clear expectations.
S – You process emotions internally and privately.

Life Through This Lens

You learned to show care by doing. So resting can feel like you're disappearing. Praise doesn't always land. You are seen as the strong one, but few know how heavy it feels. You don't show your overwhelm. You organize it. And even in exhaustion, you keep going because letting go feels more dangerous than burning out.

Where It Began

You likely grew up in an environment where competence was

expected and emotions were downplayed. You became reliable fast. Being in charge felt safer than being vulnerable.

How This Shows Up

IN CONFLICT: You keep your cool and look for solutions.

IN WORK: You are structured, responsible, and often in charge.

IN FRIENDSHIP: You show up by doing, not emoting.

IN CREATIVITY: You thrive in systems, order, and design.

IN GROWTH: You learn that rest isn't failure.

> **Reflection**: What are you afraid will fall apart if you step back?

THE DRIFTWOOD (PDRF)

Protector / Defender / Revealer / Feeler

You said yes, even though your body said no. You laughed when it was expected. You stayed until the very end because you always do. That's how love felt safest: distant, quiet, on their terms.

Core Instinct

Stay close. Don't cause waves. Feel everything.

Snapshot

Introspective and gentle, Driftwoods go with the flow on the outside, but hold rich emotional lives within. They often blend in, but you're not passive. They're attuned, perceptive, and quietly impacted by everything. And soft on purpose, but it can hurt, sometimes, to always be the one who bends.

Axes in Action

P – You protect others gently, often through presence.
D – You stay connected even when it hurts.
R – You shift and soften to maintain harmony.
F – You carry emotion close to the surface.

Life Through This Lens

You feel deeply, even when you don't say much. You sense what others need and adapt. But your own needs? Those are harder to name.

You become what the room needs, but it's lonely to feel everything and rarely be felt in return.

Where It Began

You likely learned early that staying soft meant staying hidden. Expression felt risky. You kept the peace by disappearing into it.

How This Shows Up

IN CONFLICT: You defer, deflect, or quietly withdraw.

IN WORK: You adapt easily and sense unspoken tension.

IN FRIENDSHIP: You're loyal, intuitive, and often underestimated.

IN CREATIVITY: You work from feeling; poetic, layered, emotional.

IN GROWTH: You begin to speak your wants out loud.

Reflection: If you allowed yourself to take up space, what would your life look like?

THE HARBOR (PDRS)

Protector / Defender / Revealer / Sealer

You stayed steady while everyone else fell apart. Not because it was easy, but because no one else knew how. And somehow, that became your role.

Core Instinct

Be steady. Be safe. Don't make it about you.

Snapshot

Reliable and compassionate, Harbors hold space for others to breathe. You're the calm in their storm, the one who notices, prepares, and softens. People feel safe near you.

Axes in Action

P – You protect through presence and groundedness.
D – You stay emotionally loyal even in silence.
R – You bend gently to fit what others need.
S – You rarely reveal what hurts unless it's safe.

Life Through This Lens

You're the strong one—the safe one. Even when you're breaking, you make others feel whole. You've sacrificed pieces of yourself to keep others comfortable.

Where It Began

You may have been raised to prioritize others' feelings. Your calm became a gift, but also a mask. You learned that stillness earned safety.

How This Shows Up

In Conflict: You anchor others but may silence your own truth.
In Work: You're dependable and team-oriented.

In Friendship: You're steady and kind, sometimes self-erasing.

In Creativity: You shine through subtlety and softness.

In Growth: You learn to honor your depth out loud.

Reflection: What do you wish someone would ask you?

CHAPTER 5
GROWTH WITH TYPE

N ow that you've come to know your type, we'll look at the four axes that shaped how you survived. These axes aren't categories. They're adaptive patterns; they were survival strategies that your nervous system chose long before you had words for them.

They formed in moments of silence, tension, rejection, or pressure. And while the shape they took may be unique to you, the questions beneath them are universal:

- How do I stay safe with others?
- What do I do when the connection feels threatening?
- How do I manage overwhelming emotion?
- When do I show what's real, and when do I hide it?

Each axis reflects a kind of emotional intelligence that was learned through repetition and response. And now, instead of being reflexes, these patterns are becoming visible. Noticeable in the choices you make, the tensions you feel, and the roles you slip into without thinking.

AXIS 1: PROTECTOR (P) VS. PLEASER (E)

Do I stay safe by setting boundaries,
or by staying liked?

This axis reflects your core interpersonal instincts: how you navigate closeness, conflict, and a sense of belonging. Protectors (P) create space and enforce boundaries to feel safe and in control, while Pleasers (E) seek closeness and prioritize harmony to avoid rejection or tension.

Neither is wrong, they're just different nervous system solutions to the same need—safety.

PROTECTOR PATTERN: SAFETY THROUGH CONTROL & DISTANCE

- May appear independent, self-sufficient, or guarded.
- Relies on boundaries, logic, or emotional shutdown to stay safe.
- Struggles with vulnerability or receiving help.

COPING INTELLIGENCE: Discernment, boundaries, self-containment.

RISKS WHEN OVERUSED: Isolation, mistrust, suppressed needs.

PLEASER PATTERN: SAFETY THROUGH HARMONY & LIKABILITY

- May appear helpful, agreeable, or emotionally tuned-in.
- Reads the room constantly and adapts to avoid conflict.
- Struggles with self-prioritization or saying no.

Coping Intelligence: Attunement, empathy, emotional tracking.

Risks when overused: Burnout, resentment, and invisibility.

Reflections:
Do I avoid conflict by agreeing, or shut it down by withdrawing?
Do I feel guilty setting boundaries?
Do I protect myself at the cost of closeness, or please others at the cost of myself?

AXIS 2: DEFENDER (D) VS. LEAVER (L)

When things go wrong, do I
fight for connection or prepare to go?

This axis reveals how you respond to rupture, disconnection, or perceived abandonment. Defenders (D) tend to push in and try to repair, explain, or fight to stay connected and Leavers (L) tend to pull away, detach, escape, or check out to stay safe.

Each is a valid form of protection. One stays to fix. One leaves to survive.

DEFENDER PATTERN: SAFETY THROUGH PROVING, FIXING, OR STAYING.

- Leans into conflict to regain closeness.
- Takes responsibility for relational repair.
- Often stays too long in unhealthy dynamics.

Coping Intelligence: Tenacity, loyalty, emotional endurance.

RISKS WHEN OVERUSED: Self-blame, over-functioning, stuckness.

LEAVER PATTERN: SAFETY THROUGH DETACHMENT AND ESCAPE

- Emotionally checks out or exits situations early.
- Appears composed but may be numb or avoidant underneath.
- May cut ties to avoid pain before it arrives.

COPING INTELLIGENCE: Adaptability, self-reliance, emotional distance.

RISKS WHEN OVERUSED: Chronic disconnection, loneliness, mistrust.

REFLECTIONS:
Do I feel safer trying to fix things or letting go?
Do I leave before I'm left?
Am I staying to connect or to prove my worth?

AXIS 3: REVEALER (R) VS. CONCEALER (C)

*Do I cope by sharing what's
real or hiding what hurts?*

This axis explores your instinct for emotional visibility and how much you show when things feel uncertain or unsafe. Revealers (R) share openly to process, connect, or stay honest, while Concealers (C) hold back to stay protected, private, or in control.

These aren't about honesty or secrecy. They're about safety through expression vs. safety through privacy.

REVEALER PATTERN: SAFETY THROUGH OPENNESS AND EMOTIONAL TRANSPARENCY

- Speaks quickly or directly about inner experiences.
- May overshare or expect mutual vulnerability.
- Finds peace in naming things aloud.

COPING INTELLIGENCE: Courage, truth-telling, emotional access.

RISKS WHEN OVERUSED: Oversharing, exposure, and emotional hangovers.

CONCEALER PATTERN: SAFETY THROUGH PRIVACY AND SELF-CONTAINMENT

- Keeps thoughts and feelings close to the chest.
- May downplay or delay expressing distress.
- Prefers time and trust before opening up.

COPING INTELLIGENCE: Discernment, restraint, quiet strength.

RISKS WHEN OVERUSED: Loneliness, misattunement, unmet needs.

REFLECTIONS:
Do I feel closer or more anxious after I share?
Do I regret speaking too soon, or not soon enough?
Was vulnerability modeled as dangerous or powerful?

AXIS 4: SEALER (S) VS. FEELER (F)

*Do I survive emotion by closing it
off, or by feeling it all?*

This axis illustrates how your nervous system manages emotional energy, particularly under stress. Sealers (S) contain or mute emotion, while Feelers (F) sense and express it.

Both strategies serve a regulatory function; one quiets the storm, the other rides it.

SEALER PATTERN: SAFETY THROUGH EMOTIONAL CONTROL OR SUPPRESSION

- Appears composed, logical, or emotionally restrained.
- May numb, intellectualize, or freeze under pressure.
- Tends to process internally or not at all.

COPING INTELLIGENCE: Containment, emotional clarity, reliability.

RISKS WHEN OVERUSED: Repression, physical tension, disconnect.

FEELER PATTERN: SAFETY THROUGH EMOTIONAL EXPRESSION AND ATTUNEMENT

- Feels deeply, absorbs energy from others.
- May cry easily or need to talk through feelings.
- Processes emotions actively and externally.

COPING INTELLIGENCE: Intuition, empathy, expressive honesty.

RISKS WHEN OVERUSED: Overwhelm, emotional fusion, misreading signals.

REFLECTIONS:
Do I get overwhelmed by feelings or shut them down?
When something hurts, do I talk about it or go quiet?
Do I feel "too emotional" or "too detached"?

RESPONSE PATTERN AXES IN PRACTICE

You've already gotten to know each axis, what it measures, and how it works. But these responses aren't just descriptions, they're your lived experiences. They're the shifts you feel inside when something changes in the room. The tightening in your chest. The scan you run without realizing. The calculation you make before you speak.

They're the instincts that shaped your timing, your tone, your posture, and the quiet negotiations happening in your mind and body at the same time.

What follows is here to help you recognize these intelligences when they're in motion, both in what you do and in what you feel. So you can see the precision of how you adapted, and notice when an old reflex is taking the lead.

AXIS 1: PROTECTOR (P) VS. PLEASER (E)

Reading the Room

You know when the room changes before anyone else says a word. Maybe you get louder to take up space before someone else does. Maybe you got softer to keep the peace. Either way, your nervous system learned to read the room, tracking mood shifts, relational cues, and the micro-changes in tone or posture that told you what to expect next.

This wasn't overthinking; it was pattern recognition honed in real time, often in rooms where connection and danger came in the same breath.

This type of interpersonal sensitivity is the intelligence that lives behind both boundary-setting and people-pleasing. It's what allows some to disarm conflict with charm, and others to brace against it with fire. It's the same instinct, only expressed in different directions.

When this intelligence is running, you're scanning for risk. You don't just read the room, you shape it. You sense the emotional atmosphere and try to adjust the thermostat so that no one gets burned. That skill kept you connected and protected. But it also meant that sometimes, you were working harder than anyone else just to stay in the room.

This is the intelligence of survivors who adapted quickly to keep the peace but who were rarely given the safety to rest.

REFLECTION: What emotional patterns do you still track, even when no one's asking you to?

AXIS 2: DEFENDER (D) VS. LEAVER (L)

Knowing When to Go

Some survival responses involve running toward the fire, while others involve looking for the nearest exit. Both require precision.

This axis holds a type of situational risk assessment intelligence. Giving you the ability to sense when something is unsafe, unsustainable, or no longer worth the cost. Whether you dug in your heels or disappeared into silence, you weren't just reacting. You were evaluating risk and conserving energy.

For some, this intelligence showed up as persistence and

knowing how to outlast discomfort without complaint. For others, it showed up as disappearance and knowing how to shut down, shut off, or shut up to avoid escalation or entrapment. Both are strategic. Both are valid. Both required a high degree of internal timing, assessment, and adaptability.

You may have learned how to stick it out and stay in things longer than was good for you. Or you learned how to leave before you were even missed. But either way, your system got good at calculating the emotional math of How much longer can I do this? And Is it safe to come back?

This is the intelligence of survivors who became fluent in bracing or disappearing. Not out of desire, but out of necessity, because those responses worked when little else did.

REFLECTION: What's your earliest memory of knowing it was time to stay or time to go?

AXIS 3: REVEALER (R) VS. CONCEALER (C)

Timing What you Tell

Some people tell the truth to feel safe. Others withhold it to survive. This axis holds both types of disclosure management intelligence. This is what's behind how and when you share your inner world. It's not just about honesty, it's about timing, precision, and control. You learned what to say, when to soften, and what to keep hidden.

For Revealers, this often looked like transparency used as defense, getting ahead of pain by putting it all out there. For Concealers, it often looked like holding back not to deceive, but to protect, to manage how much of your truth the world could handle at once. Neither is less brave than the other. Both required constant internal calculation.

You may still monitor how much you say in a moment of vulnerability. You may still feel exposed, even after speaking gently. You may still hear yourself sharing a story and wonder, 'Did I give too much away?' Or: Did I say enough for them to really know me?

This intelligence kept your truth safe. And in many ways, it kept you safe. The goal isn't to undo it. It's important to notice when you're using it and why.

REFLECTION: When did you first realize the world couldn't hold all of you at once?

AXIS 4: SEALER (S) VS. FEELER (F)

Holding What You Feel

This axis isn't about being emotional or not. It's about what happens when emotion becomes too much to carry. Managing the intensity of your own emotional landscape requires a type of emotional self-regulation that is intelligence.

For Feelers, that often means staying open, porous, and deeply attuned. They learned how to move through pain rather than away from it, but that often means drowning in it alone.

For Sealers, it means compressing emotion, locking it down, and keeping themselves from being overwhelmed. But that didn't mean they didn't feel it; it just meant they had to contain themselves.

This intelligence isn't visible from the outside. It shows up in how you talk to yourself in the dark. In the ways you self-soothe without language. In the quiet rituals that helped you survive intensity without making a mess of it.

REFLECTION: When alone, what do you do with big feelings?

The patterns beneath your type formed to keep you safe. They weren't flaws. They were strategies. They got you through what you didn't ask for. They helped you navigate what felt impossible but survival responses weren't meant to last forever. They were meant to help you last. And now, you have something your younger self didn't have: awareness, language, and the capacity to choose.

You already carry the answers.
Trust yourself enough to listen.

CHAPTER 6
SURVIVAL ARCHETYPES

Think of the last time you felt under pressure. Maybe your chest tightened, or you went quiet, or you started solving before anyone else knew there was a problem. That wasn't random; that was survival intelligence moving through you.

Underneath the habits and reflexes is something steadier, your archetype. It's the default pattern your nervous system adopts, forged from history, instinct, and the survival strategies that have become second nature.

Each of the Survival Response Types belongs to one of four larger Survival Archetypes. They are the emotional center of gravity, like the patterns you return to again and again, whether you notice it or not. Each carries its own emotional logic, strengths, and quiet tensions, all rooted in the ways you've learned to survive.

Think of the last time you felt under pressure. Maybe you pulled back, maybe you leaned in, maybe you disappeared into fixing before the need was even spoken. That wasn't random; that was survival intelligence moving through you.

Underneath those habits and reflexes is something steadier

—your archetype. It's the rhythm your nervous system falls back on, forged from history and instinct. Each of the Survival Response Types belongs to one of four larger Survival Archetypes. They are the emotional center of gravity you return to again and again, often without noticing. Each carries its own emotional logic, strengths, and quiet tensions, rooted in the ways you've learned to survive.

THE SENTINELS

(Protector + Sealer Types)

"If I stay in control, I won't fall apart."

Core Traits:
Sentinels are grounded, guarded, and responsible. They track danger, physical or emotional, and carry the weight of prevention. Most of their energy goes into staying ahead of risk, whether that means managing situations, holding others accountable, or silencing their own needs to stay functional.

They don't flinch easily, but they do tighten. Sentinels rarely break down; they hold tight. For others, they are the storm shelter and the checklist, the deep breath before the fall.

How Safety Was Defined:
Sentinels often learned that vulnerability was dangerous or never an option. In these households or systems that lacked safety, their nervous systems adapted by minimizing emotional output and maximizing functional strength. Essentially, sealing off emotions became a means of survival without distraction or exposure. For them, protecting others often felt easier than letting anyone protect them.

YOU STAYED CALM WHILE EVERYONE ELSE SPUN OUT. MADE THE PLAN, HELD THE LINE, KEPT IT MOVING. NO

ONE ASKED HOW YOU WERE DOING. BECAUSE THEY NEVER DO, AND MAYBE THAT'S THE POINT. YOU ALWAYS HOLD IT TOGETHER BECAUSE SOMEONE HAS TO. IT NEVER FELT LIKE YOU HAD A CHOICE.

Common Strengths

- Exceptional in crises, clear, capable, contained.
- Loyal to the people they protect, even when exhausted.
- Good at setting boundaries.
- Predictable, consistent, and emotionally solid under stress.
- Often seen as "the strong one," but not always understood.

Quiet Costs

- Tend to push away help or softness, even when they need it.
- May confuse silence with strength, and control with safety.
- Can grow resentful but struggle to express it.
- Often mistake hyper-independence for emotional maturity.

Common Blind Spots

- Believing emotional distance is safer than closeness.
- Thinking responsibility = love.
- Misreading their need to hold it together as a personality trait.

SENTINEL SUBTYPES

THE DIRECTOR (PDCS) takes charge with calm authority, often stepping into leadership roles out of necessity. Values order, logic, and precision, but may struggle to show emotional nuance. Healing begins when they start to realize not everything needs to be managed, especially their feelings.

THE HARBOR (PDRS) offers steadiness and grounding to others, especially in relationships. They are dependable and quietly loyal, but may neglect their own emotional needs for the sake of peace. Growth comes from allowing themselves to be held, not just being the holder.

THE COMMANDER (PLCS) is tactical, resourceful, and unflinching under stress. They often keep emotions locked down to prioritize survival. But over time, their armor can become suffocating. Healing starts when they learn that releasing control won't result in collapse.

THE WARDEN (PLRS) is protective, cautious, and often skeptical of emotional exposure. They may create rigid boundaries to keep chaos out, but also keep connection out. Growth means learning to soften their grip without losing their sense of safety.

THE MIRRORS

(Pleaser + Revealer Types)

"If I can feel what you feel, maybe I'll be safe in the feeling too."

Core Traits:

Mirrors are emotionally expressive, relationship-driven, and naturally attuned to the feelings of others. They often act as emotional translators, sensing what others can't say and offering connection as a way to earn safety. They're warm, responsive, and thoughtful in conversation, but may sacrifice their own needs for the sake of keeping the peace.

What looks like empathy is often a survival instinct finely tuned to avoid rupture or rejection.

How Safety Was Defined:

Mirrors learned early that emotional connection could prevent abandonment. They believe safety comes from being emotionally accessible, open-hearted, and present. Especially for others in distress. Their empathy is genuine, yet often driven by pressure to perform or over-function.

YOU NOTICED A SHIFT BEFORE ANYONE HAD SAID A WORD. IT JUST FELT SAFER TO TAKE CARE OF THE MOMENT RATHER THAN RISK BEING LEFT INSIDE IT. THE WAY THE SILENCE SCREAMED, HOW THEIR BODY LEANED AWAY. SO YOU SOFTENED, OFFERED TO HELP, AND MADE YOURSELF SMALLER. YOU DIDN'T MEAN TO DISAPPEAR.

Common Strengths

- Deep empathy and emotional fluency.
- Skilled in emotional care, mediation, and relationship-building.
- Able to sense and respond to others' emotional needs quickly.
- Create environments where people feel seen and understood.

Quiet Costs

- Emotional overextension.
- Chronic self-neglect or suppression of personal needs.
- Fragile self-worth tied to how others feel around them.
- May confuse emotional labor with love.

Common Blind Spots

- Believing they must always "show up" to be loved.
- Avoiding boundaries out of fear they'll disappoint others.
- Merging with others' emotional states, losing clarity on their own.
- Struggling to receive care without earning it.

MIRROR SUBTYPES

THE ADVOCATE (EDCF) often feels others' pain deeply and often takes on the emotional burdens of those around them. They feel safety in advocacy and moral attunement, but may struggle to protect their own emotional boundaries.

THE COMPANION (EDRF) is emotionally responsive and steady in care, but may struggle to assert autonomy. They prioritize others' needs instinctively and fear disconnection more than their own discomfort.

THE STRATEGIST (ELCF) is highly attuned to emotional nuances and is quick to detect shifts in tone or tension. Burns out from over-functioning and anticipating others' emotional needs before they're spoken.

THE MEDIATOR (ELRF)
Harmony-focused and relationally flexible, but prone

to losing themselves in others. They adapt quickly to maintain the peace, even at the cost of their own identity or their need for clarity.

THE FIRESTARTERS

(Protector + Revealer Types)

"If I don't say it, who will?"

Core Traits:
Firestarters are bold, emotionally honest, and often misread as intense. Their survival style is expressive and defensive; they don't wait for harm to arrive; they preempt it. Some fight with words, others with silence or withdrawal. What unites them is a deep belief that truth matters, and that hiding emotion is more dangerous than showing it.
They're not trying to create conflict; they're trying to create clarity in a world that punishes confusion.

How Safety Was Defined:
Firestarters often learned that if they pushed back, they stayed in control. Whether in homes where boundaries were ignored or feelings were dismissed, Firestarters came out swinging.

> YOU SAID IT CALMLY BUT FIRM ENOUGH THAT NO ONE MISSED THE EDGE. YOU WEREN'T TRYING TO START SOMETHING. YOU WERE JUST DONE LETTING THINGS SLIDE. YOU LEFT THE ROOM STILL SHAKING, WONDERING IF YOU WENT TOO FAR. BUT SOMETHING IN YOU KNEW THAT STAYING SILENT WOULD'VE COST MORE.

Common Strengths

- Honest, loyal, and emotionally brave.
- Protect others fiercely, especially the vulnerable.

- Cut through confusion or gaslighting.
- Don't mind confrontation if it protects integrity.
- Lead with intensity and passion.

Quiet Costs

- May escalate or overcorrect when feeling unsafe.
- Struggle to soften or ask for comfort.
- Emotionally exhausted from constant hyper-vigilance.
- Can unintentionally scare or overwhelm others.
- Often feel "too much" and carry deep shame about it.

Common Blind Spots

- Confusing control with safety.
- Using anger to mask fear or sadness.
- Believing they must protect others from themselves.
- Mistaking volatility for authenticity.

FIRESTARTER SUBTYPES

THE GUARDIAN (**PDCF**) is fueled by a fierce sense of duty and protection. They often express emotion through justice and defense. They are quick to step in to shield others from harm. Healing begins when they allow themselves to grieve what they couldn't protect.

THE DRIFTWOOD (**PDRF**) is emotional and intuitive, but still quick to act. They float between connection and control, often overwhelmed by their own feelings but unwilling to seal them away. Healing means learning to pause without fear of disappearing.

THE DIRECTOR (**PDCS**) is decisive and emotionally

direct; they often channel their feelings into action, in leadership or confrontation. While they aim for truth, they may overpower softer voices. Growth comes from learning that not all expression must land like a hammer.

THE RESCUER (PLRF) is responsive, caring, and ready to intervene. Their fire is aimed at fixing, saving, or helping, sometimes without being asked. Their challenge is recognizing that not all help is helpful, especially when it replaces emotional presence with performance.

THE SHAPESHIFTERS

(Leaver + Feeler Types)

"If I stay flexible, I won't break."

Core Traits:
Shapeshifters are emotionally sensitive, fluid, and fiercely adaptive. Their survival response is rooted in absorbing emotional undercurrents and adjusting quickly, often without realizing it. They learned to stay safe by shifting shape: becoming who others needed, disappearing when tension rose, or sensing their way through discomfort with subtle, strategic grace. They don't cling to roles; instead they, flow.

How Safety Was Defined:
Their nervous system learned that if I change fast enough, I won't get hurt. So they became intuitive, emotionally reactive, and masterful at sidestepping conflict. They often seem attuned and emotionally present, but they're always half-ready to disappear if things turn cold.

You could feel the mood shift before anyone spoke. So you adjusted, changed the tone, smoothed the tension, and made the moment easier to carry. No one asked you to. They never do. You're just good at making things okay. But later, you realized you hadn't said a single thing you meant.

Common Strengths

- Highly empathic, emotionally fluid, and intuitive.
- Gentle, responsive, and able to navigate relational nuance.
- Skilled at diffusing conflict or tension with tact and timing.
- Often artistic, emotionally expressive, or spiritually attuned.
- Flexible and adaptive in unpredictable situations.

Quiet Costs

- May lose track of their own needs or desires in relationships.
- Prone to emotional burnout or identity confusion.
- Tend to flee or shut down when intensity peaks.
- Struggle to hold boundaries, especially with people they care about.
- Often feel like they're "too much" and "not enough" at the same time.

Common Blind Spots

- Confusing adaptability with authenticity.
- Believing survival depends on staying small, soft, or agreeable.
- Feeling safe only when invisible or helpful.

- Mistaking sensitivity for weakness and masking it with distance.

SHAPESHIFTER SUBTYPES

THE DIPLOMAT (ELRS) is attuned, thoughtful, and emotionally perceptive. They often become the emotional barometer in relationships. Adjusting tone, words, or presence to maintain peace. Their gift is harmony, but it can come at the cost of honesty. Growth begins when they realize that clarity doesn't have to mean conflict.

THE TACTICIAN (ELCS) is quietly adaptive and strategically attuned. This subtype excels at reading the room and recalibrating in real time, often anticipating needs before they're named. Their minds move fast, but their emotions may remain hidden. Healing starts when they allow themselves to be known, not just useful.

THE ANCHOR (EDRS) is steady, supportive, and quietly intuitive. This subtype grounds others through presence rather than performance. They may avoid emotional waves by sinking deeper into stillness, but still feel everything. Growth comes from letting their own feelings surface without guilt or apology.

THE ADVISOR (EDCS) is wise, measured, and emotionally observant. This subtype often offers insight rather than intimacy, guiding others with care while keeping themselves at a distance. Their strength lies in clarity, but healing begins when they stop editing their own needs out of the conversation.

You may recognize parts of yourself in more than one archetype or feel like all of them, depending on the day. That's
okay. These patterns weren't made in a moment, and they
won't be unmade in one either.

The patterns were never random.
They were the shape your safety took.

CHAPTER 7
THE SHAPE OF SURVIVAL

You were never broken; you were adapting. Now, you're beginning to notice the instincts that kept you safe, the roles that once made sense, and the patterns that no longer quite fit.

This chapter is about what comes after awareness. For some, survival patterns formed around individual trauma. For others, they were shaped by systems—racism, ableism, poverty, medical trauma, or being in a world that wasn't built to support their needs.

What roles or reflexes once felt protective, but now feel like they cost you too much?

Each survival type learned to be excellent at something, like hyper-vigilance, emotional care, adaptability, or self-control. The problem is that their excellence was often born of fear.

They became excellent because they had to be, not because it was easy.

Which parts of your excellence were shaped by fear?
Which still feel necessary to stay safe?

This work isn't about becoming someone else. It's about feeling safe as yourself. Recognizing your early emotional logic and noticing when it activates in the present. Creating new patterns that feel safer, not scarier

That might mean grieving the version of you who had to be strong or stay silent to survive. It might mean revisiting old wounds with new eyes. Not to reopen them, but to stop organizing your life around their echoes.

AXIS 1: PROTECTOR ↔ PLEASER

This axis reflects how you seek safety in relation to power and peace. Protectors often feel safest when they're in control, and Pleasers often feel safest when others are comfortable.

If the Protector side feels familiar, you may instinctively take charge or try to control situations to prevent chaos. If the Pleaser side feels familiar: You may prioritize other people's comfort over your own needs.

You might notice your jaw tighten when someone offers feedback. Or feel the urge to take over a situation when it feels chaotic. That isn't failure. It's your nervous system remembering that being in control once kept you safe.

You noticed your grip tightening on the steering wheel, the plan, the outcome. But this time, you didn't jump in. You didn't take charge. You let someone else lead. It wasn't easy, you felt, it was exposure. But no one got hurt. And maybe, just maybe, you're allowed to rest too.

You might offer reassurance even when you're drained. Or say "yes" before checking how you actually feel.

That instinct once protected you.

You almost said yes. The word rose out of habit, already halfway formed. But your jaw clenched, and for once, you caught it. You exhaled instead. "Can I get back to you?" The room didn't freeze. No one frowned. And for the first time, your no wasn't a door closing, it was space opening.

AXIS 2: DEFENDER ↔ LEAVER

Which moments in your week reveal your relationship to power or peace?

This axis reflects how you relate to presence and distance in moments of threat. Defenders stay close, hyper-aware, and prepared. Leavers pull back to avoid overwhelm or exposure.

If the Defender side feels familiar: You may stay hyper-alert, always braced for what could go wrong. If the Leaver side feels familiar then you may detach or disappear when things get emotionally intense.

You might always be preparing or mentally rehearsing, bracing, and scanning for what could go wrong. That hyper-readiness was once necessary, but is it today?

You might emotionally disappear the moment things feel too warm, too close, too much. Leaving helps you avoid being seen as a burden.

You felt the urge to fade, to go quiet, to say you were fine, to disappear before anyone noticed. But something in you stayed. You shifted in your seat instead of leaving it. Let them see your hesitation. Let yourself be seen. The air thinned, but it didn't collapse. And you were still there.

AXIS 3: REVEALER (R) VS. CONCEALER (C)

Do you tend to brace for what's coming or disappear before it arrives?

This axis reflects how you use truth and visibility to stay safe. Revealers stay one step ahead by sharing openly. Concealers stay safe by staying hidden.

If the Revealer side feels familiar: You may speak too quickly or over-share in order to manage connection. If the Concealer side feels familiar: You may hold back, staying quiet to avoid being overwhelmed.

You might blurt out the truth before you've even processed it. You might over-explain or over-expose to manage connection. That was once how you stayed in control of your story.

You didn't plan to say it. It just slipped out, soft and half-swallowed, like you weren't sure it counted. But they didn't rush to fix it. They didn't fill the silence. They just looked at you like it was normal to be known. And for a moment, you believed them.

You might stay quiet even when it hurts. You might tell yourself it's safer not to say anything at all.

That silence was once armor.

You almost didn't send the message. You rewrote it four times, hands trembling, the weight of old silence pressing against your ribs. But you sent it, one clear sentence. Not dramatic. Not perfect. Just true. And when they wrote back with warmth, not overwhelm, something inside you softened: maybe your quiet doesn't have to mean invisible.

AXIS 4: SEALER ↔ FEELER

Are you more afraid of being too seen,
or not seen at all?

This axis reflects how you protect your inner emotional experience. Sealers contain, protect, and withhold. Feelers absorb, express, and attune to their surroundings.

If the Sealer side feels familiar: You may keep things in, struggling to open up even when it feels safe. If the Feeler side feels familiar: You may absorb the emotions of everyone around you.

You might find yourself holding back, even when part of you wants to speak. You might confuse openness with danger. That instinct kept you safe from being used or misunderstood.

You didn't explain everything. You just said, "I'm not okay." It wasn't a performance; it was a truth your body wasn't used to letting out.
They didn't press. They just nodded and stayed in the room. That was new. And your chest didn't tighten the way it usually does. You noticed the safety after. Quiet, but real.

You might feel everything, yours and everyone else's. You might try to soothe people before they even speak. That was once how you kept the peace.

You felt it before they said a word, the shift in their mood, the edge in their voice. Your body tensed to meet it, ready to smooth the air before it turned sharp. But this time, you didn't rush to fix it. You let the discomfort hang. Your hands stayed in your lap. And even though every part of you hummed with urgency, you realized: not every feeling in the room belongs to you.

THE NOTICE–NAME–NURTURE LOOP

Notice when your type is active and offer yourself a new choice, one moment at a time.

1. **NOTICE:** Pause and feel what's happening in your body. "My chest feels tight. I'm getting ready to shrink."

2. **NAME:** Gently name the pattern without judgment. "This is my Pleaser instinct, trying to keep me safe by making me smaller."
3. **NURTURE:** Offer yourself a new micro-response. "What if I took up space here, even a little? What if I let myself need something?"

This is how we build safety without strategy. Not by erasing our instincts but by reminding them they have options now.

You've begun to see the shape of your survival and how it formed, how it still moves, and what it costs you. Maybe you've even started to notice those moments in real time. Like the tightening, the shrinking, the urge to stay useful or disappear. But here's the part we often overlook in healing, survival didn't begin with thought. It began with sensation. With reflex. With your body stepping in long before your mind could explain why.

Survival began in your body.
Your mind only followed.

CHAPTER 8
SAFETY, REWRITTEN

Many survival responses weren't built in chaos, they were built after chaos. In the stillness, your body stayed ready. You adapted not just to survive a moment but to survive being you.

The problem is that your nervous system doesn't update itself once your environment changes. Even when it's safe, your body doesn't always believe it.

So it continues to do what worked when it wasn't safe.

That's why healing can feel confusing. You're not reacting to what is; instead, you're reacting to what was, or what might be. Your body doesn't use logic. It uses memory.

You may notice your shoulders tense when someone enters the room too quickly. You may freeze in a conversation that feels too honest, even if nothing's actually wrong. You may snap, shut down, dissociate, or disappear without understanding why. Sometimes, you don't even notice it until after it's already happened.

Because your nervous system is fast, faster than thoughts, and faster than words. It was built to act before your brain had time to decide. And for a long time, that kept you safe.

These moments aren't mistakes, they're signals. Your body

is trying to protect you, the only way it knows how. By reacting to what feels familiar, even when the danger is long gone.

Rebuilding safety begins with recognizing these responses, not as problems to be fixed, but as patterns to be understood.

The part of your brain holding survival patterns doesn't keep track of time. It doesn't say, "That happened years ago." It says, "This feels familiar," and launches the same old response.

This is implicit memory, the kind of memory stored not in words, but in sensations, reflexes, and patterns. You might not remember the event, but your body remembers the aftermath.

Even healing moments like stillness, closeness, and visibility can feel threatening at first. Not because they are, but because your body remembers what used to follow stillness, closeness, or visibility. Maybe honesty once led to punishment. Maybe affection was followed by abandonment. Maybe being seen meant being judged, or being helped meant owing something back.

That's why even a gentle question, "How are you really?" can make your chest tighten. Your body's not reacting to the question. It's reacting to the history it carries.

The brain isn't malfunctioning when it reacts like this. It's protecting you. Your nervous system learned to act fast and big because something once made that reaction necessary.

Survival responses like hyper-vigilance, people-pleasing, or emotional numbing are not overreactions. They are what kick in when your system believes; If I don't do this, I won't be okay.

Real safety is choice, not control. Stillness without panic, connection without performance, and visibility without shame. Survival isn't just a thought, it's a full-body memory. And the body has to be part of the healing.

This is why you can't just "think your way" into healing. If your safety has always depended on a strategy like people-pleasing, disappearing, or being useful, then real safety might feel disorienting or strange at first. It might feel boring. Scary. Like something's missing.

Understanding your nervous system is only the beginning. Awareness helps you name what's happening, but it's not the same as feeling safe. Healing doesn't come from insight alone. It comes from new experiences that slowly teach your body: this moment is different.

Feeling safe can't be rushed, it can't be forced, and you can't think your way into it. You have to build it, moment by moment, pattern by pattern. Your Survival Response Type can help you recognize the strategies that you've been using to survive, and gently explore what safety might look like for you beyond each strategy.

I was strong! Strong for everyone else. I handled the vet calls. I watched his symptoms. I camped out in the living room for weeks so he wouldn't be alone. That was my way; stay useful, stay steady, don't need anything.

I had always been the Driftwood; floating through grief, holding steady for others, never asking to be held.

I didn't expect this loss to change how I let people love me. But when Toto was dying, something in me shifted. The part of me that usually drifted quietly through crisis, steady, unobtrusive, and always adapting just couldn't stay quiet anymore. Not this time, something in me shifted.

It was small at first. I didn't shut down like I used to. I reached out. I told friends what was happening. I answered the phone. I didn't say I was fine. And people came.

My best friend heard about Toto during finals and still drove for days with my goddaughter in the back seat. Toto was sunbathing on his favorite couch, staring out the window, too big and too tired to be posed. So she worked around him— trimming his fur with quiet care, taking paw prints, snapping photos while her baby crawled across her lap.

There was so much life in the room and so much love that I still can't think about it without breaking open.

Another long-time friend had stopped by our house for a quick pitstop on the way home from his sister's funeral. Then, they stayed, unprompted, for days. The house was full of laughter that didn't feel out of place, of meals left on the counter, of people who knew how to sit with grief without needing it to be named.

For the first time, I didn't try to grieve alone. I didn't minimize it. I didn't disappear. I let people see it all. And it felt disorienting.

Letting myself receive that kind of care felt strange. Like I'd missed a step. Like I was forgetting who I was supposed to be. For so long, I'd kept people at arm's length when things got heavy, telling myself it was easier that way, safer. But this time, something shifted. Maybe because he always picked me. Maybe because, without him, I couldn't pretend I didn't need picking.

Maybe your version looks different. Maybe you stay cheerful to avoid being a burden. Maybe you disappear when things get too real. Maybe you don't know how to say, "Can you stay?" even when everything in you needs someone to. Whatever it looks like, it started as safety. But it doesn't have to end there.

Rebuilding safety doesn't mean feeling calm all the time. It means learning to recognize when you're not and gently asking yourself why.

It's not a single moment. It's a pattern, a practice, a shift. It's what happens when you stop trying to become someone lovable and start letting yourself be someone real.

Rewriting safety means unlearning the old rules: you don't need anything, you don't show anything, and you don't take up space.

It means noticing the moments you tense up or disappear, not to shame yourself but to ask, What part of me still thinks this is the only way?

And then, slowly, offering that part a new way forward.

This is where your Survival Response Type becomes a compass, not a label, but a guide. It helps you name what safety used to mean for you…and what it could mean now.

Protector
"I can trust others to help carry the load."
Pleaser
"I can stay visible, even when I say no."
Defender
"I don't need to prove my readiness."
Leaver
"I can be here without dissolving."
Sealer
"I can be known in small, safe ways."
Feeler
"I can feel fully and still stay grounded."
Revealer
"I can be honest without unraveling."
Concealer
"I can be held, not just hold others."

Each of these isn't just a statement. It's a possibility. A new groove in your nervous system. A new signal to your body that this moment is different from the one you survived.

Rebuilding safety doesn't mean erasing who you've been. It means letting yourself belong to this version of you, the one who doesn't have to perform strength to be protected. The one who's learning that safety isn't earned through usefulness. It's offered through presence.

The way we build safety in ourselves quietly shapes how we show up with others.

CHAPTER 9
THE LANGUAGE OF SURVIVAL

We all speak a kind of emotional shorthand, one shaped not just by what we believe, but by what we've survived.

Before we learn to say "I love you," we learn how to stay safe. We learn to soften our needs. Not with words but with patterns. We tighten. We please. We fix. We disappear.

These patterns don't vanish in adulthood; instead, they speak for us, especially in the moments that matter most. Each survival type tends to default to certain behaviors when stress, vulnerability, or a sense of connection arises.

These patterns become our survival languages, our ways of expressing care, fear, apology, or closeness without ever having to say them out loud.

But here's the problem: survival languages don't always translate. What one person means as connection can land as control. What feels like self-protection to one may feel like abandonment to another.

Because love isn't just about what you say, it's about what your nervous system is trying to say underneath.

Most relational conflict isn't about what happened; it's about how you felt and what it meant to your nervous system.

That's why two people can walk into the same moment and experience completely different realities. One person hears, "I need space," and feels a sense of relief. The other hears abandonment. One person offers to help, and it lands as love. Another offers to help, and it lands as control.

This is the hidden layer in nearly every relationship: We're not reacting to each other. Each of us carries a set of deeply ingrained response patterns that once helped us survive discomfort, chaos, or disconnection.

In relationships, these patterns don't just vanish; they become how we ask for closeness, how we signal danger, how we mask our needs, or how we disappear when we feel threatened.

We're reacting to what our survival responses think is happening.

Every survival type speaks its own emotional language when stress hits. In the next section, we'll explore how all eight types express safety, fear, love, and how those messages often get lost in translation.

Your Survival Response Type doesn't only show up when you're alone. It shows up in conversation, in conflict, in silence.

It shows up when you're trying to avoid being "too much". Or managing other people's moods. Maybe you feel shame for needing anything to are trying to feel safe without feeling exposed.

Each type carries unspoken beliefs about safety, love, and worth. We don't always know we believe them, but we live like they're true. They often sound like this:

- **PLEASER:** If they're upset, I've failed.
- **DEFENDER:** If I let my guard down, I'll be attacked.
- **LEAVER:** If I stay, I'll disappear.
- **SEALER:** If they see too much, they'll leave.
- **FEELER:** If I don't absorb it, they'll fall apart.

- **Revealer:** If I'm not fully honest, I'm not real.
- **Concealer:** If I show myself, I'll be rejected.

These are adaptations, not flaws. They're like a map drawn by your nervous system to help you survive relationships. Relationships that once felt dangerous, uncertain, or overwhelming.

When we're overwhelmed or hurt, we don't always say what we mean.

Each type's survival language is the way they try to stay connected or safe when they feel threatened or emotionally exposed.

We default to what's familiar, our survival language.

Each of the four axes in this framework represents a survival pattern, but in relationships, those patterns also become languages. The way we express love, fear, and need often comes through our earliest emotional dialects, ways of being that helped us stay safe.

THEY ASKED WHAT WAS WRONG, AND YOU SAID, "I'M SORRY." NOT BECAUSE IT WAS YOUR FAULT, BUT BECAUSE THAT'S WHAT YOUR BODY LEARNED TO SAY WHEN THINGS FELT OFF. BEFORE YOU EVER LEARNED TO ASK FOR WHAT YOU NEEDED, YOU LEARNED TO SHRINK. THAT WAS YOUR LANGUAGE. THAT HAD ALWAYS BEEN YOUR LANGUAGE.

Understanding these languages helps prevent a common relational wound, like misreading a protective gesture as a personal attack.

AXIS 1: PROTECTOR ↔ PLEASER

The Protector may feel like the Pleaser is sugarcoating or not taking things seriously. The Pleaser may feel like the Protector is harsh or unkind when both are trying to help in the only way they know.

Protector
Love = loyalty, action, fierce protection.

- "I'll fix it." "I've got your back." "I'll take care of it.".
- May come off as controlling, blunt, or impatient.
- Beneath it: fear of helplessness or powerlessness.

Pleaser
Love = softness, attunement, harmony.

- "Are you okay?" "What do you need?" "I just want you to be happy."
- May come off as vague, avoidant, or overly accommodating.
- Beneath it: fear of conflict or being rejected for having needs.

AXIS 2: DEFENDER (D) ↔ LEAVER (L)

The Defender feels abandoned when the Leaver walks away, and the Leaver feels trapped or smothered by the Defender's insistence on resolving.

Defender
Love = staying, proving, holding steady.

- "Let's talk now." "We can work through this.".
- May come off as pressuring or codependent.
- Beneath it: fear of being left or discarded.

Leaver
Love = space, preservation, autonomy.

- "I need to cool off." "I'll talk when I'm ready.".
- May come off as cold, distant, or unavailable.
- Beneath it: fear of emotional overwhelm or engulfment.

AXIS 3: REVEALER (R) ↔ CONCEALER (C)

The Revealer feels dismissed by the Concealer's retreat. The Concealer feels exposed by the Revealer's openness.

Revealer
Love = openness, truth-telling, transparency.

- "I want to talk about everything." "I need to say what I feel.".
- May come off as invasive or intense.
- Beneath it: fear of being shut out or deceived.

Concealer
Love = discretion, privacy, protection of self.

- "I don't want to talk about it." "I'm not ready.".
- May come off as secretive or disengaged.
- Beneath it: fear of vulnerability being weaponized.

AXIS 4: SEALER (S) ↔ FEELER (F)

The Sealer feels overwhelmed when the Feeler pours everything out. The Feeler feels dismissed when the Sealer holds everything in.

Sealer
Love = quiet consistency, not burdening others

- "I'm fine." "It's no big deal." "I'll handle it.".

- May come off as cold, distant, or uncaring.
- Beneath it: fear of being too much or making others uncomfortable.

Feeler

Love = emotional honesty, visible connection.

- "This hurts." "I need you to see me.".
- May come off as dramatic or needy.
- Beneath it: fear of emotional invisibility.

When people argue, they rarely say what they mean. They say what their nervous system needs to say to feel safe. Some shut down. Some blow up. Some try to keep the peace. Some walk away mid-sentence and never look back.

These are not just communication habits; they're relational survival strategies.

In the heat of conflict, we all tend to reach for our most practiced form of protection. However, naming your response in real-time can reduce escalation and invite deeper empathy. It's not about perfection, it's about pattern awareness.

Examples

A Protector in conflict might say: *"This is ridiculous. Just let me handle it."*
But underneath, they're thinking: *"If I don't take charge, this will fall apart."*

A Leaver might walk away mid-argument and not come back for hours. Not because they don't care, but because their body equates staying with danger.

A Sealer may feel the tears rising and bury them in chores. Because they were once taught: don't let anyone see you break.

LOVING SOMEONE IN SURVIVAL MODE

When someone you love is in survival mode, it doesn't always look like pain. It doesn't always look like panic or shutdown; sometimes it looks like doing everything "right."

High-functioning survival strategies like high achievement, relentless helpfulness, emotional silence, or always being the one who keeps it together can be just as rooted in fear as collapse or withdrawal.

They're harder to name, because they're often rewarded. But underneath, they still carry the same ache. I don't feel safe being fully seen here.

And when you love someone like that, especially while they're healing. It can be both deeply meaningful and deeply exhausting.

You will sometimes feel shut out, misread, or emotionally orphaned. Not because your partner doesn't love you but because their nervous system still struggles with letting love in.

- You are not responsible for fixing your partner's survival patterns.
- But you can become a safer landing space.
- That means you don't force change.
- You model safety.
- You hold the door open and name what you see.
- You choose curiosity over defensiveness.
- And when it gets too heavy, you take care of yourself, too.

REPAIR & RECONNECTION

No relationship exists without rupture. Words are said that can't be unsaid, and tones land harder than intended. One person goes quiet. The other grows louder. And both walk away feeling misunderstood.

But rupture isn't the enemy; avoiding repair is.

Sometimes the best repairs aren't big talks. They're the quiet offerings that say, "I still choose you." Maybe it's a hand on the shoulder, or a shared inside joke. A plate of food placed nearby or a text that says, "still here."

When survival has trained you to expect abandonment or betrayal, these gestures feel like little miracles. Like proof that love can stay even when it's hard.

Some relationships teach us pain, but others become the first place where we learn to feel safe. Not because there's no conflict, but because there's repair.

That's what turns survival into healing, not escaping the past, but rewriting it.

Survival turned the ordinary heavy.
Healing makes it light again.

CHAPTER 10
SURVIVAL IN DAILY LIFE

U nderstanding how your survival response took shape can bring clarity. But what matters just as much is noticing how it still shows up and beginning to make gentler choices, one moment at a time.

By now, you've seen how survival types form and what they carry. The next step is recognizing how those patterns play out in daily life, like how they show up in leadership, work, friendship, and creativity.

The Survival Response Type Indicator isn't just a framework; it's a compass. It helps you spot the moments where survival might still be in the driver's seat, so you can begin to steer in a new direction.

PROTECTOR (P)

- **LEADERSHIP**: Leads boldly but may dominate or interrupt when feeling unsafe.
- **WORK**: Takes charge but may struggle with collaboration or listening.
- **FRIENDSHIP**: Fiercely loyal, may be seen as intense or defensive in conflict.

- **CREATIVITY**: Creates bold, uncompromising work but may resist feedback.

PLEASER (E)

- **LEADERSHIP**: Builds harmony but avoids conflict or hard decisions.
- **WORK**: Eager to help, often says yes at their own expense.
- **FRIENDSHIP**: Loyal friend but struggles to express needs or set boundaries.
- **CREATIVITY**: Creative voice may shift to please others instead of staying true.

DEFENDER (D)

- **LEADERSHIP**: Endures stress well, may resist change or over-function.
- **WORK**: Stays too long in draining roles, avoids asking for help.
- **FRIENDSHIP**: Stays in unhealthy dynamics out of loyalty or duty.
- **CREATIVITY**: Pushes through blocks but may force output rather than flow.

LEAVER (L)

- **LEADERSHIP**: Cool under pressure but can emotionally disengage.
- **WORK**: Independent, may be seen as distant or uninvolved.
- **FRIENDSHIP**: Disappears in emotional seasons even when they care.
- **CREATIVITY**: Thrives in solitude, avoids feedback or co-creation.

SEALER (S)

- **LEADERSHIP**: Composed, reliable leader, but may miss emotional cues.
- **WORK**: Prefers structure and clarity, avoids emotional labor.
- **FRIENDSHIP**: Cares deeply but rarely shows it, hard to read emotionally.
- **CREATIVITY**: Creates refined work but avoids expressive risk.

FEELER (F)

- **LEADERSHIP**: Leads with empathy, risks burnout from emotional overload.
- **WORK**: Deeply tuned into team emotions, absorbs stress.
- **FRIENDSHIP**: Emotionally generous, sometimes overwhelmed by others' needs.
- **CREATIVITY**: Creates with depth but resists structure or revision.

REVEALER (R)

- **LEADERSHIP**: Models vulnerability, may overshare under pressure.
- **WORK**: Initiates connection, may reveal too much too soon.
- **FRIENDSHIP**: Bonds fast, may later regret how quickly they open up.
- **CREATIVITY**: Creates to connect, but overexposure may lead to burnout.

CONCEALER (C)

- **LEADERSHIP**: Strategic, self-contained, may be seen as guarded or aloof.
- **WORK**: Loyal and observant, avoids being seen or spotlighted.
- **FRIENDSHIP**: Hard to read, slow to trust, but deeply loyal when safe.
- **CREATIVITY**: Creates in secret, fears judgment or exposure.

Survival responses don't just show up in trauma; they show up in trust. And friendship is one of the most vulnerable places we reveal—or hide—ourselves. Understanding your type can help you recognize how you connect with others, and what might be running in the background when things get tough.

PROTECTOR (P)

- **HOW YOU CONNECT:** You defend your people like they're family.
- **WHEN STRESSED:** You may escalate, overreact, or push people away to regain control.
- **WHAT YOU NEED:** Friends who honor your loyalty without fearing your fire.

PLEASER (E)

- **HOW YOU CONNECT:** You anticipate others' needs and earn love through helpfulness.
- **WHEN STRESSED:** You overextend, over-apologize, or disappear in shame.
- **WHAT YOU NEED:** Friends who notice you, not just what you do for them.

DEFENDER (D)

- **How you connect:** You stay through storms and show love by showing up.
- **When stressed:** You may suppress needs, stay too long, or collapse in private.
- **What you need:** Friends who check in and don't assume you're always okay.

LEAVER (L)

- **How you connect:** You're independent but loyal once trust is earned.
- **When stressed:** You ghost or emotionally disengage to protect your energy.
- **What you need:** Friends who accept that distance isn't a disinterest.

SEALER (S)

- **How you connect:** You're calm, steady, and tend to understate your affection.
- **When stressed:** You may seem emotionally unavailable or unreadable.
- **What you need:** Friends who don't demand expression but still make space for you.

FEELER (F)

- **How you connect:** You sense others' emotions deeply and care intensely.
- **When stressed:** You absorb pain, withdraw, or feel emotionally saturated.

- **WHAT YOU NEED:** Friends who support without offloading and remind you you're not a fixer.

REVEALER (R)

- **HOW YOU CONNECT:** You open up quickly and crave mutual vulnerability.
- **WHEN STRESSED:** You may overshare, test loyalty, or regret opening too fast.
- **WHAT YOU NEED:** Friends who honor your emotional courage and give you space to recalibrate.

CONCEALER (C)

- **HOW YOU CONNECT:** You build trust slowly and reveal yourself over time.
- **WHEN STRESSED:** You retreat into silence or act fine while unraveling.
- **WHAT YOU NEED:** Friends who are patient, observant, and never force the door.

Leadership isn't just about titles; it's about how we shape our environment, make decisions, and respond under pressure. Survival shows up here too—not only in crisis, but in how we earn trust, hold authority, and carry the weight of responsibility. Some types lean in. Others retreat. All are trying to stay safe. This isn't about becoming a "better" leader, but a more aware one, so your instincts don't lead the room when your values should.

PROTECTOR (P)

- **HOW YOU LEAD:** You take the lead instinctively and assertively.

- **WHEN STRESSED:** You may micromanage, bulldoze, or fight unseen threats.
- **WHAT YOU NEED:** To pause before protecting everyone from discomfort.

PLEASER (E)

- **HOW YOU LEAD:** You prioritize team harmony and emotional safety.
- **WHEN STRESSED:** You avoid confrontation, over-accommodate, or burn out quietly.
- **WHAT YOU NEED:** To believe that leading doesn't mean being liked by everyone.

DEFENDER (D)

- **HOW YOU LEAD:** You're steady under pressure and loyal to the mission.
- **WHEN STRESSED:** You over-function, suppress needs, or resist necessary change.
- **WHAT YOU NEED:** To trust that stepping back isn't abandoning the team.

LEAVER (L)

- **HOW YOU LEAD:** You observe first and act with cool detachment.
- **WHEN STRESSED:** You may become disengaged, indifferent, or checked out.
- **WHAT YOU NEED:** To stay emotionally invested even when uncertainty spikes.

SEALER (S)

- **HOW YOU LEAD:** You value logic, clarity, and consistency.
- **WHEN STRESSED:** You default to control, policy, or emotional restraint.
- **WHAT YOU NEED:** To invite emotional nuance without losing stability.

FEELER (F)

- **HOW YOU LEAD:** You lead with empathy and emotional awareness.
- **WHEN STRESSED:** You may absorb the team's stress or feel responsible for everyone's pain.
- **What you need:** To lead with heart and boundaries.

REVEALER (R)

- **HOW YOU LEAD:** You lead through connection and shared vulnerability.
- **WHEN STRESSED:** You may over-share or make emotional decisions prematurely.
- **WHAT YOU NEED:** To ground openness with discernment.

CONCEALER (C)

- **HOW YOU LEAD:** You lead through preparation, quiet strength, and observation.
- **WHEN STRESSED:** You may become rigid, withdrawn, or emotionally unreadable.

WHY WE SURVIVE THE WAY WE DO

- **WHAT YOU NEED:** To let people see enough of you to trust where you're leading.

Work is often where our survival strategies speak the loudest. Whether it's staying late, staying silent, or staying hyper-visible, these patterns shape how we navigate teams, deadlines, and demands. We're not just earning paychecks—we're managing perception, energy, and emotion.

PROTECTOR (P)

- **HOW YOU WORK:** You take charge, drive results, and guard your team.
- **WHEN STRESSED:** You may react defensively, resist collaboration, or take over.
- **WHAT YOU NEED:** Environments that value your initiative without feeding urgency.

PLEASER (E)

- **HOW YOU WORK:** You anticipate needs and strive to be indispensable.
- **WHEN STRESSED:** You overcommit, over-function, and burn out silently.
- **WHAT YOU NEED:** Work cultures that honor limits as much as loyalty.

DEFENDER (D)

- **HOW YOU WORK:** You're dependable and will carry the weight when others drop it.
- **WHEN STRESSED:** You hide struggle, avoid change, and over-identify with responsibility.
- **WHAT YOU NEED:** Permission to rest without guilt and to be supported, not just leaned on.

LEAVER (L)

- **How you work:** You're self-sufficient and calm under pressure.
- **When stressed:** You detach, avoid visibility, or emotionally check out.
- **What you need:** Space to process, but structure that keeps you engaged.

SEALER (S)

- **How you work:** You're clear, organized, and value doing things the right way.
- **When stressed:** You may resist feedback, avoid ambiguity, or over-control.
- **What you need:** Flexibility that feels safe and colleagues who read between the lines.

FEELER (F)

- **How you work:** You tune into the team's emotional current and try to ease it.
- **When stressed:** You absorb tension and feel personally responsible for everyone's morale.
- **What you need:** Emotional clarity, not just emotional labor.

REVEALER (R)

- **How you work:** You connect quickly, bring passion, and infuse meaning into tasks.
- **When stressed:** You may overshare, struggle with boundaries, or feel raw and exposed.

- **WHAT YOU NEED:** Safe containers for expression and structured emotional pacing.

CONCEALER (C)

- **How YOU WORK:** You're consistent, thoughtful, and prefer to fly under the radar.
- **WHEN STRESSED:** You go quiet, suppress feedback, and feel unseen.
- **WHAT YOU NEED:** To be invited, not interrogated, and recognized without pressure.

And then there's creativity. Vulnerable by nature, it's not just about talent or output; it's about letting something true come through you. For many people, especially those with survival-based adaptations, that feels like a risk.

PROTECTOR (P)

- **How YOU EXPRESS:** Boldly, with intensity and conviction.
- **WHEN BLOCKED:** You may over-control, critique harshly, or fear appearing weak.
- **WHAT FREES YOU:** Letting creativity be messy instead of mastered.

PLEASER (E)

- **How YOU EXPRESS:** In ways that please, soothe, or impress others.
- **WHEN BLOCKED:** You may fear judgment, seek too much feedback, or play it safe.
- **WHAT FREES YOU:** Creating without an audience in mind.

DEFENDER (D)

- **How you express:** With depth and dedication, especially when it helps others.
- **When blocked:** You may feel unworthy of creating for yourself.
- **What frees you:** Making space for joy, not just usefulness.

LEAVER (L)

- **How you express:** Thoughtfully and with restraint.
- **When blocked:** You may minimize your ideas or disengage entirely.
- **What frees you:** Releasing the need to get it just right before starting.

SEALER (S)

- **How you express:** With precision, structure, and control.
- **When blocked:** You may censor emotion or fear imperfection.
- **What frees you:** Trusting emotion as part of the process, not a flaw in it.

FEELER (F)

- **How you express:** Through deep, emotional currents, often intuitive and raw.
- **When blocked:** You may feel too exposed or overwhelmed by your own feelings.

- **WHAT FREES YOU:** Knowing your emotions are signals, not threats.

REVEALER (R)

- **How YOU EXPRESS:** Openly, vulnerably, and with a desire to be seen.
- **WHEN BLOCKED:** You may share too soon or shut down after rejection.
- **WHAT FREES YOU:** Protecting your process until it's ready, not hiding, just healing.

CONCEALER (C)

- **How YOU EXPRESS:** Quietly, subtly, and with deep intention.
- **WHEN BLOCKED:** You may keep your creativity entirely private, or never act on it.
- **WHAT FREES YOU:** Allowing others to see the edges of your truth, one piece at a time.

Every type carries its own way of moving through daily life, but beneath them all is the same longing—to feel safe enough to show up as we are.

Survival kept me half-present.
Healing lets me arrive whole.

CHAPTER 11
SURVIVAL AT THE SURFACE

B y now, you've likely started to notice how the survival response type manifests and how it manifests through your habits, silence, and efforts to hold it all together. These responses formed in silence, in tension, in the places where words never reached. They aren't flaws. They're answers your body rehearsed when it had no choice but to adapt. They are the strategies that kept you here.

When you step back, you may notice that all survival responses trace back to the same set of questions:

- How do I stay safe with others?
- What do I do when connection feels threatening?
- How do I manage overwhelming emotion?
- When do I show what's real, and when do I hide it?

Your responses to these questions might not have felt like choices. They were reflexes, wired into you long before you knew what they meant. Each axis reflects a kind of lived emotional intelligence. Learned through repetition and response. And now, instead of being reflexes, these patterns are becoming visible.

You've seen how survival carries itself in different places of life, and how it holds, how it hides, how it helps, and what it costs.

Let what you've recognized sit with you. You don't need to turn it into action right away. Noticing is enough. The more you see these patterns, the less they move unseen. And when they're not unseen, they're no longer the only language you have.

THE STRATEGIST (ELCF)

Pleaser / Leaver / Concealer / Feeler

Core Instinct
Stay ahead. Stay calm. Stay useful.

IN CONFLICT
You respond by managing. When tension rises, you shift into strategist mode, organizing, fixing, and anticipating outcomes before anyone else reacts. You rarely lose your cool. However, that calm often comes at a cost, such as emotional detachment, internalized pressure, and a sense that you're only as safe as you are useful.

"I don't need to win, I need it not to fall apart."

IN WORK
You lead with clarity and foresight.

You're deeply competent and emotionally attuned, often the one holding things together. You plan five steps ahead and make it look effortless. But when others rely on you without reciprocation or overlook your emotional labor, you may burn out quietly, unsure how to ask for help without losing value.

Strength: Emotional intelligence meets operational skill

Strain: Over-functioning masked as leadership

IN FRIENDSHIP
You show care by solving.

You anticipate what others need and offer it before they ask. You're the planner, the one who remembers details, the quiet anchor. But you may feel unseen if others don't notice how much energy you're spending. It can be hard to let people see the mess underneath your control.

"I don't want to be needed, I want to be known."

IN CREATIVITY
You build systems with soul.

You're drawn to meaningful structure like writing that guides, tools that heal, frameworks that clarify. You may struggle to start if the vision isn't clear or if emotional expression feels indulgent. But when you allow vulnerability into your structure, your work becomes a lighthouse.

Purpose-driven. Thoughtful. Quietly powerful.

IN GROWTH & HEALING
You begin by releasing the need to hold everything. Healing doesn't mean letting go of your strengths; it means letting them serve you, not control you. You grow when you realize usefulness isn't your worth. You're allowed to rest. You're allowed to not know. You're allowed to be loved outside of what you do.

Let others in, not to help them, but to be helped in return.

"My value is not measured by what I manage."

THE TACTICIAN (ELCS)

Pleaser / Leaver / Concealer / Sealer

Core Instinct
Stay useful. Stay composed. Don't get messy.

IN CONFLICT
You go quiet and try to fix.

Your first instinct is containment. You scan for what's broken, what needs solving, and you get to work. You rarely raise your voice, but you may silence your feelings in the name of peace. You fear that expressing too much could make things worse, so you trade emotion for efficiency.

"If I stay calm, maybe this won't fall apart."

IN WORK
You're the backbone.

You're organized, reliable, and exacting. You keep things running in the background, rarely needing praise. You make people feel safe because you always have a plan in place. But you may take on too much, believing it's your role to fix what others fumble, even when it drains you.

Strength: Dependability with structure
Strain: Hidden burnout from invisible repair work

IN FRIENDSHIP
You support through action.

You're loyal and practical, showing up early, remembering details, and fixing what others overlook. But you may struggle to open up, fearing you'll burden the people you love. You're present in crisis, but hesitant when it comes to your own vulnerability.

"I'm here.
I just don't always know how to be seen."

IN CREATIVITY
You create with precision and care.

You prefer grounded forms like design, systems, and tools. You value clarity and utility in your creative work. Emotional expression may feel risky or inefficient, but when you let softness slip in, your work becomes quietly moving.

Clean lines. Honest rhythm. Structure as self-expression.

IN GROWTH & HEALING
You begin by naming what you feel, before trying to fix it.

Healing means letting the chaos in without needing to immediately contain it. You grow when you allow your feelings to surface, even when they're messy. Being steady is your gift, but you don't have to hide behind it.
Your stillness can include your softness.

"I am allowed to feel, not just function."

THE MEDIATOR (ELRF)

Pleaser / Leaver / Revealer / Feeler

Core Instinct
Keep the peace. Keep everyone okay.

IN CONFLICT
You absorb and accommodate.

You read the room before you speak. You sense emotional shifts like weather and adjust your presence accordingly. When conflict arises, you de-escalate by softening, agreeing, retreating, or appeasing; sometimes before you even know what you feel.

"I'll disappear a little if it helps keep the peace."

IN WORK
You're the relational glue.

You anticipate team needs, manage tension, and carry out emotional labor that others may not even notice. Your adaptability makes you invaluable, but you may be so attuned to others that your own direction becomes blurry. You work best in environments that feel emotionally safe.

Strength: Harmonizing teams and dynamics
Strain: Losing your voice in group settings

IN FRIENDSHIP
You listen with your whole body.

You remember what others forget, show up when it matters, and adapt to different emotional landscapes with grace. But you may struggle to name your needs, fearing they'll disrupt harmony. You want to be chosen, but sometimes settle for being needed.

"I'm always there for them. I just wish

I knew if they'd be there for me."

IN CREATIVITY
You create from feeling.

Your work is intuitive, responsive, and relational. You're drawn to softness, tone, and emotional resonance. You may delay sharing your creations out of fear they'll cause tension or seem self-indulgent, but when you speak, your truth ripples.

Subtlety as expression. Emotion as clarity.

IN GROWTH & HEALING
You begin by asking: What do I want?

You grow when you stop shapeshifting for approval and start rooting in your own wants. Your care for others doesn't need to disappear, but your voice matters, too. You're allowed to hold space without disappearing inside it.

Let your truth be part of the harmony.

"My needs are not a disruption, they're a direction."

THE ADVOCATE (EDCF)

Pleaser / Defender / Concealer / Feeler

Core Instinct
Protect others. Hold it together.

IN CONFLICT
You step in to help, sometimes too fast.

When emotions run high, you instinctively try to fix, soothe, or shield others from harm. You're often the one people turn to. But when no one turns to you, the weight builds. You may carry guilt when others hurt, even when it's not yours to hold.

"If I can't help, what good am I?"

IN WORK
You lead with compassion and conviction.

You're steady, dependable, and invested in people's well-being. You naturally take on invisible labor, often becoming the go-to person in a crisis. But you may forget to pause, often burning yourself out in the name of being useful.

> **Strength:** Deep responsibility fused with heart
> **Strain:** Overextension without boundaries

IN FRIENDSHIP
You love by showing up.

You're the one who remembers, checks in, offers solutions and emotional support. You often feel more comfortable giving than receiving. You may struggle with resentment when others don't reciprocate the depth of care you offer.

"I'll carry it for them. I always have."

IN CREATIVITY
You express what needs defending.

Your work may reflect justice, grief, healing, or hope. You're drawn to meaning and purpose. When you allow vulnerability into your art, beyond what's helpful to others. It becomes a powerful act of self-recognition.

IN GROWTH & HEALING
You begin by turning your care inward.

You grow when you stop rescuing as a substitute for connection. You are more than what you do for others. Healing means recognizing that you are worthy of the same compassion you give so freely.

You don't need to hold everyone to be held.

"I am not only a helper.
I am a human who also deserves help."

THE ADVISOR (EDCS)

Pleaser / Defender / Concealer / Sealer

Core Instinct
Stay steady. Stay helpful. Don't need too much.

IN CONFLICT
You ground the room without saying much.

You rarely escalate. You listen, assess, and try to understand before responding. You may focus on fixing the problem rather than naming your own feelings. Conflict makes you uncomfortable, not because you fear it, but because it feels inefficient or unnecessary.

"If I stay calm, maybe they will too."

IN WORK
You're a quiet stabilizer.

You show up early, do the work, and anticipate needs others miss. You rarely demand attention but are often essential to the team. You find comfort in systems and rhythm, but may resist change that threatens your sense of control.

Strength: Steadfast clarity and quiet execution
Strain: Over-functioning while being under-recognized

IN FRIENDSHIP
You offer loyalty, not messiness.

You're the person others confide in. You give guidance, show up consistently, and rarely ask for anything in return. You may seem distant emotionally, not because you don't care, but because needing things makes you feel vulnerable or exposed.

> *"I don't want to be a problem.*
> *I want to be the one people can count on."*

IN CREATIVITY
You create through refinement and structure.

You're drawn to order, elegance, and thoughtful design. You may avoid raw expression, favoring composed and purposeful output. Your work often reflects clarity, integrity, and crafts-manship.

Still waters, deep clarity. Meaning through precision.

IN GROWTH & HEALING
You begin by admitting your own needs exist.

You grow when you realize you don't have to be the strong one all the time. Healing means allowing others to support you, even when it feels uncomfortable. Steadiness isn't just what you offer; it's something you deserve to receive, too.

Let being held be part of your wisdom.

> *"My needs matter, even when I stay quiet about them."*

THE COMPANION (EDRF)

Pleaser / Defender / Revealer / Feeler

Core Instinct
Stay close. Stay soft. Stay useful.

IN CONFLICT
You soothe instead of speak.

You instinctively tune into other people's pain. In tense moments, you lean toward reconciliation, softening your tone, adjusting your presence, absorbing discomfort to maintain closeness. But sometimes you quiet your own truth just to stay connected.

"If I can stay soft, maybe they'll stay too."

IN WORK
You lead with heart and harmony.

You build trust slowly and care deeply about group dynamics. You're emotionally attuned and quietly protective of others' well-being. But you may over-function to maintain connection, and avoid leadership roles that might put you at odds with people you care about.

> **Strength:** Relational depth and intuitive support
> **Strain:** Over-accommodation and difficulty asserting boundaries

IN FRIENDSHIP
You're present, tender, and deeply loyal.

You offer your whole heart, often without asking much in return. You listen more than you speak and instinctively adjust to others' moods. But your generosity can become self-erasure if your needs are constantly deprioritized.

"If I make it easier for them to stay,
I'll never be alone."

IN CREATIVITY
You create with warmth and longing.

Your work reflects connection, care, and emotional resonance. You're drawn to intimacy in art, stories, music, or tactile mediums that reflect softness and truth. Your creativity shines when it's allowed to feel, not just serve.

Emotionally guided. Beauty through tenderness.

IN GROWTH & HEALING
You begin by asking: What is mine to carry?

You grow when you reclaim your desires without apology. Healing means learning that love doesn't have to be earned through usefulness, and connection doesn't require self-sacrifice. You are allowed to be loved as you are, not just for what you give.

Let closeness include you, too.

"I am allowed to need, not just nurture."

THE ANCHOR (EDRS)

Pleaser / Defender / Revealer / Sealer

Core Instinct
Keep everyone steady, even if I sink.

IN CONFLICT
You absorb tension to calm the room.

You rarely raise your voice. Instead, you center others by softening your own presence. You sense emotional storms early and try to ground people with stability. But you may internalize pain, staying silent even when you're hurting.

"If I stay calm, maybe things won't fall apart."

IN WORK
You are the quiet glue that holds everything together.

You show up, hold the line, and carry what needs to be carried. You're emotionally reliable and highly perceptive but unlikely to voice needs or concerns unless pressed. You prefer order and may resist chaos by downplaying your own struggle.

Strength: Grounded presence in high-stress environments
Strain: Suppressed emotion and quiet overextension

IN FRIENDSHIP
You're deeply loyal but rarely ask for help.

You're the safe one, the steady friend others lean on. You remember birthdays, show up in crises, and quietly anticipate needs. But when you're struggling, you tend to hide it to avoid disrupting the peace you've worked so hard to protect.

"If I'm not the steady one, who will be?"

IN CREATIVITY
You express through calm, rooted forms.

Your work may feel quiet on the surface, but underneath,

there's depth. You prefer subtlety and resonance over drama. You might be drawn to mediums that reflect stillness, earthiness, or long-form expression.

Creative stillness. Depth beneath simplicity.

IN GROWTH & HEALING
You begin by recognizing your own inner tide.

You grow when you stop shrinking your needs to stay balanced. Healing means trusting that your presence matters even when it shakes. Your steadiness is powerful, but it doesn't need to cost your truth.

Let others hold the weight sometimes, too.

"I can be steady without silencing myself."

THE PILLAR (PLCF)

Protector / Leaver / Concealer / Feeler

Core Instinct
Keep everyone warm, but don't burn too bright.

IN CONFLICT
You retreat without leaving.

When tension rises, you stay close but guarded. You may offer calm, supportive energy without revealing your inner world. You tend to regulate yourself so others don't have to. If conflict feels emotionally unsafe, you'll withdraw quietly, even if you're still physically present.

"If I stay soft and small, no one gets hurt."

IN WORK

You show up with quiet consistency.

You are intuitive, thoughtful, and protective of the team's emotional undercurrent. You often perform invisible emotional labor, tracking the group tone and offering support behind the scenes. But you may feel unseen or underappreciated in systems that reward assertiveness over sensitivity.

> **Strength:** Loyal presence and emotional attunement
> **Strain:** Quiet burnout from emotional over-monitoring

IN FRIENDSHIP

You're a deeply loyal listener.

You remember the small things. You sense when something's off before anyone says it aloud. You offer a safe space but rarely take it for yourself. You may hesitate to share when you're hurting, afraid of being seen as a burden.

"I'll hold your pain. I'm not sure where to put mine."

IN CREATIVITY

You create from emotional texture.

Your work often reflects nuances of grief, empathy, and beauty. You may be drawn to layered forms: photography, songwriting, reflective storytelling. You craft emotion into meaning, often with restraint and power.

Art as insight. Gentleness as strength.

IN GROWTH & HEALING

You begin by letting yourself be seen.

You grow when you stop hiding the depth of your care. Healing means allowing your tenderness to come forward without apology. You don't have to protect others from your truth; it's not too much.

You are allowed to shine without shrinking.

"My gentleness is not a liability, it's a gift."

THE COMMANDER (PLCS)

Protector / Leaver / Concealer / Sealer

Core Instinct
Take charge. Shut it down. Keep it moving.

IN CONFLICT
When things heat up, you pivot to action. You cut through chaos, clarify next steps, and contain emotion before it slows you down. You may come across as dismissive or blunt, but underneath is a deep desire to protect others from emotional fallout, even if it means sealing off your own.

"Let's fix it before it gets messy."

IN WORK
You lead with clarity, decisiveness, and results.

You take ownership naturally and are rarely rattled under pressure. You thrive in structured environments and often become the go-to when crises arise. However, you may struggle with delegation or vulnerability, equating competence with a sense of control.

Strength: Clear direction and command presence
Strain: Emotional distance and over-responsibility

IN FRIENDSHIP
You're reliable, but rarely soft.

You show love through problem-solving, protection, or practical help. You'd rather act than emote, and others may misinterpret this as coldness. You care deeply, but rarely say it out loud. Letting people see you without your armor can feel unfamiliar.

"I'll take care of it. That's how I show I care."

IN CREATIVITY
You build with precision and purpose.

You're drawn to systems, strategy, and creation with impact. You may resist messier forms of self-expression unless they serve a clear goal. Your work often carries structural clarity, sharp focus, and quiet authority.
Order as expression. Power without excess.

IN GROWTH & HEALING
You begin by loosening your grip.

You grow when you allow space for emotional complexity, not just action. Healing means realizing that vulnerability isn't weakness and that control isn't the only path to safety. Your presence is powerful, but your softness matters too.

You don't have to do it all alone.

"My strength includes softness; I don't have to earn safety through control."

THE RESCUER (PLRF)

Protector / Leaver / Revealer / Feeler

Core Instinct
Help now. Feel later. Fix it fast.

IN CONFLICT
You rush to solve before you're ready to feel.

You move toward distress with immediacy, instinctively trying to mend what's broken. You offer care before it's asked for, sometimes even before you realize you've offered it. If your efforts aren't received, you may withdraw completely, feeling invisible or unappreciated.

"If I don't help, who will?"

IN WORK
You thrive in crisis but may burn out in calm.

You're reliable, responsive, and emotionally aware. You act quickly when someone's hurting, often without being asked. But you may neglect your own needs in the process, confusing value with self-sacrifice. You're proud of your impact but tired of being the one who always steps in.

Strength: Empathy in motion, fast emotional triage
Strain: Overextension and emotional depletion

IN FRIENDSHIP
You're the first to show up and the last to ask for help.

You listen deeply, support fiercely, and often take on more than your share. But when you're the one struggling, you hesitate. You don't want to burden anyone. Your loyalty runs deep, but your silence can feel like a form of abandonment.

*"I know how to care.
I'm still learning how to be cared for."*

IN CREATIVITY
You create from urgency and feeling.

You may be drawn to expressive, emotionally raw forms of writing, advocacy, spoken word, or narrative storytelling. Your creativity often centers around justice, empathy, or healing. You speak from the wound, not just the scar.

Art as balm. Expression as action.

IN GROWTH & HEALING
You begin by pausing.

You grow when you stop rushing to fix what hurts and start tending to your own pain with the same urgency. Healing means learning that your worth isn't in your output and that help is not your only identity.
You are more than what you offer others.

"I deserve the same care I so freely give."

THE WARDEN (PLRS)

Protector / Leaver / Revealer / Sealer

Core Instinct
Stay quiet. Stay safe. Watch everything.

IN CONFLICT
You go still and scan for danger.

You rarely react immediately. Instead, you retreat inward, analyze, and decide if it's worth revealing how you feel. You may say little, but you notice everything. If trust has been broken or things feel performative, you'll quietly withdraw to preserve your peace.

"Silence is safer than saying something I'll regret."

IN WORK
You bring calm, focus, and quiet integrity.

You prefer structure and solitude over chaos or emotional noise. You lead by example, not fanfare. You're careful with your energy and rarely ask for support, even when you need it. You're often respected but misunderstood.

> **Strength:** Focused, principled, and quietly reliable
> **Strain:** Isolation, suppressed emotion, and misread intentions

IN FRIENDSHIP
You show care through protection, not performance.

You're loyal, observant, and emotionally present, but few people get to see your full inner world. You reveal yourself slowly and only in spaces that feel truly safe. Others may call you distant, but they don't always know what it costs you to stay visible.

"I'm here.
I'm just not ready to speak yet."

IN CREATIVITY
You express through precision and metaphor.

You may prefer writing, design, architecture, or other structured, detail-oriented mediums. You process your world in layers and symbols. Art becomes a safe place to be fully known, without revealing too much.

Truth behind walls. Depth in control.

IN GROWTH & HEALING

You begin by risking small visibility.

You grow when you let safe people into the places you usually protect. Healing means learning that discernment isn't isolation and that you can reveal parts of yourself without losing control.

Not everything sacred needs to stay hidden.

"I can be safe and still be seen."

THE GUARDIAN (PDCF)

Protector / Defender / Concealer / Feeler

Core Instinct

Step in. Hold strong. Keep others safe.

IN CONFLICT

You move to protect before anyone asks.

You don't flinch when things get hard; you buckle down. You absorb emotion, manage logistics, and shield the vulnerable. But you may override your own needs and expect others to hold themselves to your standard of resilience. If people crumble, you'll carry them. If you crumble, you'll hide it.

"I've got this. I always do."

IN WORK

You operate like emotional armor.

You take on more than your share, lead with focus, and protect your team from unnecessary chaos. Others rely on your steadiness but rarely ask how you're holding up. You may struggle with delegation and feel responsible for things far beyond your role.

Strength: Strong presence, protective leadership
Strain: Silent burnout and internalized pressure

IN FRIENDSHIP
You offer unwavering loyalty but hesitate to lean.

You show love through acts of protection, commitment, and steadiness. You're often the one others rely on, but when you need something, you may not ask. You fear being a burden or appearing weak. Love feels safest when you're giving it.

"I'm here for you, just don't worry about me."

IN CREATIVITY
You build with purpose and durability.

Your creativity tends to have structure and weight. You may be drawn to building systems, movements, or work that serves others. Even your most personal expressions may carry a sense of service, legacy, or meaning.

Art as impact. Creation as care.

IN GROWTH & HEALING
You begin by letting yourself be carried.

You grow when you recognize that strength isn't always silent, and that being supported doesn't make you less capable. Healing means loosening your grip and trusting that others won't drop you.

You are worthy of rest without having to earn it.

"I don't have to be the strong one to be safe."

THE DIRECTOR (PDCS)

Protector / Defender / Concealer / Sealer

Core Instinct
Stay focused. Stay in control. Don't drop the ball.

IN CONFLICT
You stay composed, sometimes to a fault.

When emotions run high, you tighten your focus and take charge. You solve the problem, contain the fallout, and rarely show how much it affects you. You may struggle to express vulnerability, often defaulting to action over emotion.

"Let's keep this on track."

IN WORK
You're the backbone of every operation.

You're structured, pragmatic, and exceptionally reliable. You lead quietly and effectively, often carrying more than others realize. But you may conflate productivity with worth, and struggle to rest unless everything is resolved.

> **Strength:** Steady, strategic, and clear-headed
> **Strain:** Over-responsibility and emotional detachment

IN FRIENDSHIP
You show up through action, not expression.

You're the one who organizes, handles logistics, and solves problems. You're loyal but guarded. Others may feel cared for but not always emotionally connected to you. Letting people in means risking being seen without the structure.

"You don't need to ask, I've already taken care of it."

IN CREATIVITY
You thrive in structured expression.

You're drawn to systems, design, or work with clear rules and outcomes. Even when creative, you often filter your ideas through function and purpose. You may resist creative risks that feel untested or overly personal.

Clarity as beauty. Order as safety.

IN GROWTH & HEALING
You begin by softening your grip on control.

You grow when you allow imperfection, rest, and emotional honesty. Healing means knowing that you're still worthy when you're not managing everything and that presence matters more than performance.

You're allowed to be held, not just depended on.

"I am enough, even when I step back."

THE DRIFTWOOD (PDRF)

Protector / Defender / Revealer / Feeler

Core Instinct
Stay close. Don't cause waves. Feel everything.

IN CONFLICT
You bend instead of breaking.

You tend to go quiet, soften your edges, and absorb tension without pushing back. You may defer, deflect, or disappear to avoid making things worse. Your sensitivity helps you navigate discomfort, but it also makes it hard to know when to stand your ground.

"If I stay soft, maybe this will pass."

IN WORK
You adapt easily but rarely assert.

You're intuitive, responsive, and attuned to the undercurrents that others miss. You often know what a room needs before anyone else does, but you hesitate to speak up unless you're sure it's safe. You may feel underestimated or underutilized.

Strength: Quiet insight and relational awareness
Strain: Self-silencing and emotional over-absorption

IN FRIENDSHIP
You offer presence, not performance.

You listen more than you speak. You feel deeply, love quietly, and are often the emotional historian in your relationships. However, your needs can get lost beneath your attunement to others, and you may become emotionally overwhelmed.

"I want to be close, but not if it disrupts the peace."

IN CREATIVITY
You create with sensitivity and soul.

Your work may be lyrical, layered, or emotionally evocative. You often express what's hard to say directly, like grief, wonder, or longing. But your creativity may get blocked when you doubt your voice or fear rejection.

Art as whisper. Expression as permission.

IN GROWTH & HEALING
You begin by claiming your space.

You grow when you stop shrinking to preserve peace and start listening to your own wants. Healing means recognizing that gentleness is strength and that your voice is worth hearing, even when it trembles.

You don't have to disappear to keep the connection.

"I am allowed to take up space."

THE HARBOR (PDRS)

Protector / Defender / Revealer / Sealer

Core Instinct
Be steady. Be safe. Don't make it about you.

IN CONFLICT
You stay calm but disappear inside.

When tension rises, you anchor others with your presence, not your voice. You de-escalate without escalating. You listen, hold space, and absorb emotion. But you may silence your own truth, afraid that expressing it would disrupt the peace you work so hard to preserve.

"I'll carry it, just please don't let this fall apart."

IN WORK
You are the steady rhythm that holds things together.

You're loyal, responsible, and attuned to others' needs. You're often the first to help and the last to ask for help. You keep teams grounded, but may suppress your ideas or downplay your worth.

> **Strength:** Quiet reliability and emotional grounding
> **Strain:** Self-erasure and unspoken overwhelm

IN FRIENDSHIP
You're the calm in their storm.

You listen deeply, love loyally, and rarely make it about you. Others may feel safe around you, but not always know you. You want connection, but hesitate to reveal emotion unless invited and trusted.

> *"I'll be here.*
> *I just don't want to take up too much room."*

IN CREATIVITY
You shine through softness and subtlety.

Your work may be quiet, emotive, and deeply sincere. You don't seek to impress, only to connect. You may express through writing, music, or acts of service. But your creativity can stall if you don't believe your voice matters.

Emotion as anchor. Simplicity as depth.

IN GROWTH & HEALING
You begin by honoring your own depth.

You grow when you let your presence matter not just for others, but for yourself. Healing means learning that you're not just a safe harbor for everyone else, you're also worthy of being seen, known, and held.
Being quiet isn't the same as being small.

"My stillness has value and so do I."

WISDOM OF SURVIVAL

Whatever Survival Response Type you are, the survival responses you developed made sense and kept you the same. Maybe it was the way your body braced, or the way you learned to scan for danger. All of it was proof that you knew how to live through what you never should have had to.

But survival was never meant to be your whole story. Naming your survival patterns doesn't erase them or the events that forged them, but it does give you something new: choice. Not the pressure to reinvent yourself, but the choice of a slow return to who you've always been, under that armor.

Some of what you've carried will stay with you, and some of it can be set down. The difference now is that you get to make the decision. That choice will shape how you meet the world: how you love, how you rest, how you speak, and how you begin again.

You've already proven that you know how to endure. The invitation now is to live safely and openly. To carry what is yours, and no more. To let your body soften into a state of safety. To trust that you belong here, without having to earn it.

And when the weight feels lighter, when you find yourself breathing without bracing, when you notice moments of quiet that used to be filled with noise, that's not survival anymore.

That's you, staying.
That's you, living.

CHAPTER 12
MORE THAN SURVIVAL

Your survival made sense. Every instinct, every silence, every effort to hold it all together was intelligence at work. It was never weakness. It was never failure. It was your body doing exactly what it was built to do: protect you.

But survival always comes with a cost. The constant scanning. The effort of smiling with a hollow chest. The way you disappear into roles and responsibilities until you can't even feel your own edges. Survival kept you safe, but it also kept you alone. It taught you to carry everything without being carried yourself.

Survival was never meant to be your the whole story. It kept you here, yes—but healing asks for something different. Healing asks you to soften, to open, to trust that your worth is not measured in how much you can carry alone.

That is the work now—not erasing the patterns, but noticing them. Not forcing yourself into someone new, but loosening the grip survival has had on your every move.

Your nervous system remembers. It holds both the storms and the shelters you've known. And while it may still react as if danger is here, awareness changes everything. You can pause. You can choose. You can offer your body the safety it never had the chance to know.

Survival built its own kind of shelter, but one with locked doors. It kept you moving, kept you useful, kept you unseen. It was safety bought at the price of loneliness.

But here, on the other side of naming it, is the beginning you've been circling toward—the moment when survival stops being the only language. The moment you risk reaching, or letting in, or being carried instead of always carrying.

For me, that beginning came the moment before my hardest goodbye. I reached for help while Toto was still here, and in that reaching I found what survival alone had never given me: proof that I didn't have to hold it all by myself.

Maybe yours will arrive in a different shape. In the trembling moment before you say what you've never said. In the softness of letting someone stay. In the pause where you choose rest over performing. In the silence where you stop explaining yourself and simply exist. However it comes, it will come.

Because survival was never the end of your story. It was the bridge. The locked doors may have kept you safe, but they also kept you waiting. And when they open—when you risk stepping through—you'll see what survival could never give you: the possibility of being known, carried, and loved exactly as you are.

That's where this book leaves you. Not with a demand to change overnight, but with an invitation: to notice, to soften, to risk opening the door. Your survival was the key that got you here. What comes next is yours to write.

You carried yourself this far.
Now you are allowed to be carried, too.

FURTHER READING BY TYPE

No one heals in a straight line. This book is designed to help you recognize the response patterns of your nervous system, identify the emotional logic of your survival, and begin to move with greater awareness and self-trust.

But once you know your type, you might wonder: where do I go from here?

The following book suggestions are here to support the specific challenges and strengths of your Survival Response Type. These books mirror your type, challenge your blind spots, and offer new paths into softness, power, rest, and regulation.

Most readers will only need one or two to begin with. Follow your curiosity, not a checklist. Healing is a personal journey, and these books serve as companions, not instructions.

Regardless of your type, you deserve
tools that speak your language.

FOUNDATIONAL BOOKS FOR ALL:

The Body Keeps the Score
— by Bessel van der Kolk

You may not remember every moment that shaped your survival, but your body does. This book serves as a foundational resource for understanding how trauma resides in the nervous system and subtly influences the instincts, patterns, and protections explored throughout. With clinical depth and compassionate storytelling, van der Kolk maps out how survival responses become hardwired—and how healing begins when we listen to the body's signals, rather than over-riding them. For every type, this book offers the why beneath the what and serves as a deeply validating starting point for reclaiming choice.

What Happened to You?
— Dr. Bruce Perry and Oprah Winfrey

You weren't born broken. You adapted. This book offers a gentle, story-rich conversation about how your early experiences shaped the way you survive. If *The Body Keeps the Score* is the map, *What Happened to You?* is the companion, walking beside you with warmth, safety, and clarity. For anyone who begins to ask, "Where did this come from?" this is a compassionate place to start.

The Deepest Well
— Dr. Nadine Burke Harris

Some patterns didn't start in adulthood; they started with survival in childhood. This book explores how early adversity shapes health, identity, and emotional regulation later in life. Grounded in both personal story and science, *The Deepest Well* helps individuals of any type connect the dots between their history and their nervous system, reminding them that healing is not just possible, but deserved.

My Grandmother's Hands
— Resmaa Menakem

Some survival isn't just yours, it's inherited. This book expands the trauma conversation to include the embodied realities of racialized and intergenerational pain. With somatic practices and grounded wisdom, *My Grandmother's Hands* offers healing not just for individuals, but for lineages. For types whose survival is shaped by ancestral weight or systemic harm, this book offers a path toward mending what lives in the body.

THE DRIFTWOOD (PDAF)

Anchored: How to Befriend Your Nervous System Using Polyvagal Theory
— by Deb Dana

For Driftwoods who feel everything and often carry it alone, this book offers a gentle way home to your body. Dana's voice is calm, relational, and grounded in science, yet never cold. It teaches you how to recognize the subtle cues of your nervous system without judgment and begin to build safety that doesn't require disappearing. If you've spent your life adapting to others, this is an invitation to anchor inside yourself.

Wintering: The Power of Rest and Retreat in Difficult Times
— by Katherine May

This is not a how-to; it's a quiet permission slip. For the Driftwood who has floated between roles, emotions, and seasons of self-loss, *Wintering* reminds you that retreat isn't failure. It's part of the rhythm. With poetic language and soft pacing, May's book validates your need for solitude, rest, and retreat without shame and gives shape to the in-between places you often inhabit.

The Language of Emotions
— by Karla McLaren

For Driftwoods who sense everything but often struggle to name their inner experience, this book offers a grounded, intuitive approach to emotional clarity. McLaren provides language for what's been felt but unspoken, validating the emotional sensitivity Driftwoods carry and helping them stay present with their feelings without losing themselves in the process.

No Bad Parts
— by Richard Schwartz

Driftwoods often adapt by becoming whatever is safest, leaving parts of themselves behind in the process. This introduction to Internal Family Systems offers a gentle way to recognize and reclaim those parts, without judgment. Schwartz's approach is compassionate, spacious, and ideal for Driftwoods learning to honor every version of themselves as part of a coherent whole.

The Wisdom of Your Body
— by Hillary L. McBride

Many Driftwoods learned early to disconnect from their bodies to survive emotional intensity. This book offers a steady, trauma-informed path back to embodied presence. McBride's tone is both clinical and deeply human, making this a meaningful resource for those ready to rebuild self-trust and stay grounded in themselves without needing to disappear.

THE GUARDIAN (PDCF)

Set Boundaries, Find Peace
— by Nedra Glover Tawwab

Guardians are often the ones who carry it all, quietly, relentlessly, and without asking for help. This book offers more than boundary advice. It's a lifeline for those who confuse love with over-responsibility. Tawwab's clear, no-nonsense tone balances compassion with structure, helping you untangle where protection became overextension and where you get to choose yourself, too.

"The Art of Showing Up"
- by Rachel Wilkerson Miller

You're dependable, loyal, the one that others lean on. This book meets the Guardian where they often hide: in their habit of showing up for others while quietly erasing themselves. With practical tools and warm encouragement, it helps you redefine presence, not as sacrifice, but as something mutual, chosen, and whole.

"The Emotionally Absent Mother"
- by Jasmin Lee Cori

For Guardians who stepped into the role of caretaker before they ever felt truly cared for, this book brings clarity to what was missing and how those absences shaped your instinct to over-function. Cori's tone is clinical yet validating, helping you recognize where your strength began as a survival response and how to offer yourself the emotional presence you've always given others.

Laziness Does Not Exist
— by Devon Price

Guardians often pride themselves on being dependable, pushing through fatigue, guilt, or discomfort to stay useful. This book challenges that belief at its root. With a research-backed tone that's both rebellious and kind, Price gives Guardians permission to rest without apology, and to redefine productivity in a way that includes their own well-being.

What Happened to You?
— by Bruce D. Perry & Oprah Winfrey

You've spent your life showing up for others, but when did anyone ask what shaped your ability to do that? This book offers a compassionate, science-informed look at how survival patterns form early and quietly. For Guardians reconnecting with the child inside their protector, it's a deeply affirming reminder: your instincts made sense, and healing doesn't require you to stop caring, only to include yourself in the care.

THE TACTICIAN (ELCS)

Permission to Feel
— by Marc Brackett

As a Tactician, you move through life with precision. You keep things running smoothly, manage quietly, and rarely let emotions interrupt your function. But just because you've learned to file emotion away doesn't mean it isn't still shaping you. This book offers a gentle, science-backed invitation to reconnect with what you've suppressed not for drama, but for clarity, safety, and choice. Emotion doesn't have to derail you. It can help you lead yourself home.

Burnout: The Secret to Unlocking the Stress Cycle
— by Emily and Amelia Nagoski

You get things done. You anticipate needs before they're

spoken. And you do it all while keeping yourself out of the spotlight. However, holding everything together comes at a cost, and this book names it with humor, heart, and practical insight. For the Tactician who powers through but feels quietly frayed, *Burnout* offers science and sisterhood to help you finally close the stress loops you never realized were still running.

The Mountain Is You
— by Brianna Wiest

You're always climbing toward goals, expectations, and solutions. But have you ever paused to ask what's driving the climb? This book meets Tacticians where they often live: in high-functioning motion that quietly masks unresolved pain. With poetic clarity and fierce compassion, Wiest helps you decode self-sabotage not as weakness, but as a survival strategy and offers a path to transform it without losing your edge.

Emotional Agility
— by Susan David

You know how to adapt, to perform, to stay ahead of what might go wrong. But emotions don't disappear just because you move fast. This book is a gentle, research-based invitation to navigate hard feelings without suppressing or over-identifying with them. For Tacticians learning to make space for discomfort without letting it derail them, David's voice is steady, practical, and empowering.

No Bad Parts
— by Richard Schwartz

You've learned to compartmentalize: the efficient self, the helpful self, the one who keeps things running. But what about the parts you've hidden to survive? This book introduces Internal Family Systems with clarity and warmth, helping

Tacticians understand that every part of themselves, even the ones that feel inconvenient or emotional, has value. You don't have to function at the cost of feeling. This is your invitation to integrate, not exile.

THE STRATEGIST (ELCF)

Atlas of the Heart
— by Brené Brown

As a Strategist, you've likely spent years mapping other people's emotions while staying just outside your own. This book offers a language-rich invitation to step in. Brené Brown helps name what you often intuit but struggle to claim for yourself, giving structure to feeling and clarity to complexity. If you've ever longed for a way to stay both emotionally intelligent and emotionally present, this book builds the bridge.

Radical Acceptance
— by Tara Brach

You're composed. Capable. Always managing the moving parts. But underneath that steadiness is a quiet fear of what might surface if you stop performing calmly. This book meets that fear with radical kindness. Tara Brach's voice is steady and expansive, guiding Strategists like you to soften control not by letting go of care, but by offering it inward, at last.

The Places That Scare You
— by Pema Chödrön

You've mastered calm. You stay steady when others spiral. But what happens when fear isn't something to manage, only something to feel? This book meets Strategists at their emotional edge: the place where composure becomes a cage. With warmth and simplicity, Chödrön invites you to stop analyzing and start inhabiting—even the parts that feel messy or uncertain. You don't have to perform peace. You can live it.

Bittersweet
— by Susan Cain

You notice what others miss: the flicker of emotion beneath words, the pain behind perfection. But you rarely let yourself dwell there. This book is for Strategists who've carried quiet sorrow while staying visibly composed. Cain offers a tender reframe: that longing, melancholy, and even heartbreak are not flaws in the system but proof of your depth. For those learning to feel without flinching, this is a map for emotional permission.

The Wisdom of the Enneagram
— by Don Richard Riso & Russ Hudson

You understand people. You read between the lines. But have you taken the same inventory of yourself? This book offers Strategists a framework rich enough to hold your nuance and direct enough to challenge your blind spots. With grounded insight and practical exercises, it helps you move from monitoring who you think you should be to reconnecting with who you already are.

THE MEDIATOR (ELRF)

Adult Children of Emotionally Immature Parents
— by Lindsay C. Gibson

If you grew up scanning the emotional tone of the room before you even knew how to name your own feelings, this book will feel like someone finally seeing behind the curtain. It offers language for why you always feel responsible, even when you know you shouldn't and, helps Mediators begin the hard but healing work of separating care from self-erasure.

Self-Compassion: The Proven Power of Being Kind to Yourself
— by Kristin Neff

You're kind to everyone, except yourself. This book is your mirror and your medicine. With research-backed tools and a deeply gentle voice, Neff offers Mediators a way to stop measuring their worth by how well they ease other people's discomfort. You don't have to disappear to be good. You just have to stay with yourself, even when it's hard.

The Language of Emotions
— by Karla McLaren

You feel everything, but naming what's yours can be the hardest part. This book offers Mediators a map for navigating the emotional waters they've spent a lifetime swimming through. With clarity and compassion, McLaren teaches you how to understand your feelings without being overwhelmed by them. For those who've been fluent in others' emotions but mute to their own, this is a powerful invitation to reclaim your inner voice.

How to Be Loving
— by Danielle LaPorte

You've made gentleness your superpower, but often forget to include yourself in that gentleness. This book invites Mediators to reroute all that care inward. With poetic insight and a soft spiritual lens, LaPorte offers reminders that your worth isn't earned through sacrifice. It's inherent. For the parts of you still waiting for permission to rest, to feel, to matter, this book is a quiet, radiant yes.

THE DIPLOMAT (ELAS)

Nonviolent Communication
— by Marshall Rosenberg

As a Diplomat, you've likely mastered the art of de-escalation: speaking gently, holding tension, and diffusing conflict before it erupts. But what happens when your needs never make it into the room? This book offers a way to express yourself clearly and compassionately, without sacrificing peace. It's not about confrontation, it's about finally letting your truth be part of the conversation.

Quiet: The Power of Introverts in a World That Can't Stop Talking
— by Susan Cain

You know how to hold space. You think before speaking. You'd rather listen than perform. *Quiet* is a love letter to that strength. For Diplomats who've felt overlooked or underestimated because they lead from stillness, this book reframes your temperament not as a limitation but as a deeply needed form of presence in a noisy world.

The Boundary is You
— by Jessica Moore

You've made peace your priority, but not always your home. This book gently teaches Diplomats how to create boundaries that feel like safety, not shame. For those who flinch at confrontation or worry that saying "no" will break the connection, Moore offers a way forward: boundaries as a form of self-honoring, not as a means of distance.

THE ADVOCATE (EDCF)

Complex PTSD: From Surviving to Thriving
— by Pete Walker

You've spent your life holding steady for others, anchoring chaos, absorbing pain, staying loyal. This book doesn't just explain trauma. It honors the quiet heroism of those who survived by protecting everyone else. For Advocates, it offers a clear, validating path out of emotional over-responsibility and into self-reclamation.

The Empath's Survival Guide
— by Judith Orloff

You feel everything and often carry what isn't yours. This book gives you the tools to set boundaries without abandoning your care. Written for those who lead with heart but live on the edge of burnout, it helps Advocates learn the difference between feeling with someone and taking it all on alone.

You Don't Have to Carry It All
— by Paula Faris

You're the one who shows up, even when you're running on empty. This book speaks directly to Advocates who've internalized the idea that their worth is tied to how much they can hold. With relatable stories and permission-laced prose, Faris offers a counter-narrative: strength doesn't mean carrying everything alone. You get to set it down.

Drama Free
— by Nedra Glover Tawwab

You've protected others from chaos your whole life, some-times even at the cost of your peace. This book is for the

Advocate learning to set limits with emotionally unpredictable people. Tawwab's voice is firm yet compassionate, helping you recognize that boundaries aren't rejection; they're a repair.

The Great Exhaustion
— by Alessandra Pigni

You care deeply. You stay longer. You burn quietly. Written for helpers, healers, and humanitarians, this book explores burnout from an emotional care perspective, offering Advocates a thoughtful, reflective space to explore what sustainable service really looks like when self-preservation isn't optional, but sacred.

THE ADVISOR (EDCS)

Maybe You Should Talk to Someone
— by Lori Gottlieb

You're the one others come to for advice, for steadiness, for clarity. But inside, there's more going on than most people ever see. This memoir peels back the polished exterior and gently explores what happens when the helper finally asks for help. For Advisors, it offers a rare and welcome mirror: a story about holding space for others while learning to take up some yourself.

The Gifts of Imperfection
— by Brené Brown

You're reliable. Responsible. Unshakeable, until you're not. This book is a kind invitation to loosen your grip on perfection and let yourself be seen, even if that means being a little messy. For Advisors who've tied worth to being composed and capable, Brown's message is both challenge and comfort: you don't have to be flawless to be loved.

The Perfectionist's Guide to Losing Control
— by Katherine Morgan Schafler

You've built a life on precision and composure, but underneath, it's exhausting. This book doesn't ask Advisors to abandon excellence. Instead, it reframes perfectionism as a misunderstood survival response. With insight and warmth, it helps you make room for creativity, flexibility, and even joy without compromising your high standards.

Platonic: How the Science of Attachment Can Help You Make—and Keep—Friends
— by Marisa G. Franco

You're the steady one. The reliable one. But sometimes the connection feels just out of reach. This book meets Advisors where they often struggle: navigating emotional intimacy in friendships. Backed by science but rooted in care, it offers practical ways to deepen connection without compromising boundaries or authenticity.

Tired As F*ck
— by Caroline Dooner

You do what needs to be done, always. But what happens when doing becomes surviving? With irreverent humor and hard-won wisdom, Dooner calls out the burnout cycle that high-functioning types often normalize. For Advisors who are tired of being the strong one, this book offers permission to stop proving and start resting.

THE COMPANION (EDAF)

Codependent No More
— by Melody Beattie

You love deeply. You listen well. You hold others with tenderness, sometimes at the cost of holding yourself. This book names the patterns you've carried without blame and offers a way to untangle love from self-abandonment. For Companions who've defined themselves through what they give, this is a guide to remembering what you need.

How to Do the Work
— by Nicole LePera

Healing can feel overwhelming, especially when you're used to focusing on everyone but yourself. This book offers a grounded, integrative path toward self-awareness and emotional sovereignty. For Companions ready to stop pouring from an empty cup, it's a step-by-step invitation to become someone who belongs to yourself, too.

Boundary Boss
— by Terri Cole

You're the one others count on. You sense their needs before they speak. But who does that for you? This book helps Companions untangle guilt from boundaries and learn that protecting your energy isn't selfish, it's sacred. With a strong yet supportive voice, Cole offers language and steps to say no without shutting down your care.

The Needs Book
— by Mara Glatzel

You care for others instinctively, but what about your needs? This book meets Companions where they often disappear: in the assumption that needing less makes them easier to love. With nurturing clarity, Glatzel shows you how to honor your needs without apology and how tending to yourself makes your care more sustainable, not less.

THE ANCHOR (EDRS)

Rest Is Resistance: A Manifesto
— by Tricia Hersey

You hold things together for teams, for families, for emotional rooms that would otherwise collapse. But your calm doesn't mean you're okay. This book is a bold and nourishing permission slip to step out of survival performance and into rest. For Anchors who've made stillness a gift to others, it's a radical invitation to claim it for yourself.

The Highly Sensitive Person
— by Elaine N. Aron

You feel more than you show. You notice what others miss. And sometimes, it's exhausting. This book validates your sensitivity not as fragility, but as deep perception. For Anchors who've stayed composed to avoid overwhelm, it offers understanding and tools to honor your nervous system without apology.

The Myth of Normal
— by Gabor Maté

You've worked hard to hold it all together, but at what cost? This book unpacks how our society normalizes disconnection from self in the name of survival. For Anchors who've buried their overwhelm to stay composed, Maté offers a compassionate call to name pain without shame and reconnect with the deeper truths your nervous system has been holding all along.

The Wisdom of Your Body
— by Hillary L. McBride

You've learned to regulate, to endure, to hold space, but what about feeling safe enough to be held? This book invites Anchors back into their bodies, not to fix what's broken, but to finally listen. With gentleness and depth, McBride offers ways to access rest, embodiment, and internal validation, especially for those who've stayed strong for too long.

Try Softer
— by Aundi Kolber

You've been taught to try harder, push through, and keep it all together. But healing isn't about effort, it's about gentleness. This book meets Anchors with the tone they rarely offer themselves: soft, affirming, and paced. Kolber's approach helps you recognize when self-control becomes self-abandonment and offers practical ways to reconnect with compassion and capacity.

THE PILLAR (PLCF)

It Didn't Start with You
— by Mark Wolynn

You carry emotions that don't always feel like your own, loyalties, grief, and fears that run deeper than memory. This book helps make sense of that weight. For Pillars who inherited emotional responsibility without explanation, it offers language for what's been living in the background, and tools to begin releasing what was never yours to hold.

Braving the Wilderness
— by Brené Brown

You're the one others count on, steady, kind, composed. But belonging doesn't always feel mutual. This book speaks to the loneliness of being emotionally available while still feeling unseen and unappreciated. For Pillars learning to stop shrinking their truth in the name of harmony, it's a guide to standing inside your life, soft, strong, and fully present.

The Origins of You
— by Vienna Pharaon

You carry more than your own story. This book helps Pillars trace the early emotional templates that taught them to endure quietly, hide their needs, and shoulder emotional burdens without complaint. Pharaon's tone is clinical yet warm, ideal for Pillars learning to step out of inherited roles and begin tending to the self beneath the strong exterior.

No Bad Parts
— by Richard Schwartz

You've learned to manage yourself by compartmentalizing. This book, rooted in Internal Family Systems, offers a framework to make peace with those inner parts not by silencing them, but by finally listening. For Pillars who keep emotional chaos locked away to protect others, Schwartz offers a new kind of leadership: one where you guide from within, not through suppression.

What My Bones Know
— by Stephanie Foo

You've been composed for so long that even your grief feels quiet. This memoir breaks that silence. For Pillars who've felt emotionally invisible even while carrying the weight of intergenerational pain, Foo's story offers validation, representation, and raw truth. It's not just about trauma, it's about finding your voice in a world that never asked for it.

THE COMMANDER (PLCS)

Dare to Lead
— by Brené Brown

You lead with clarity. You handle what others avoid. But behind all that competence is a quiet discomfort with being seen emotionally, not just functionally. This book challenges the idea that strength means staying sealed. For Commanders, it's a bridge between leadership and courage, not just in what you do, but in how you let yourself be known.

When the Body Says No
— by Gabor Maté

You don't slow down unless your body forces you. You override discomfort, push through stress, and compartmentalize pain to keep things working. But over time, your body keeps the score. This book speaks directly to Commanders who've treated emotion as a distraction and helps you understand how unmet needs and suppressed stress can take root in your health.

The 5 Personality Patterns:
— by Steven Kessler

You've mastered action. You read the room, take the lead, and keep things from falling apart. But have you ever wondered what's driving all that effort? This book offers a lens into patterned nervous system responses and how your strength may actually be a survival stance. For Commanders, Kessler provides language for what lies beneath competence and how to shift from control to choice.

Learning to Love Yourself
— by Gay Hendricks

You excel at responsibility, but what about self-regard? This book is a warm, foundational guide to self-acceptance for high-functioners who feel safest when performing. For Commanders who have built an identity on reliability and logic, Hendricks offers a deceptively simple but profound invitation: not just to love what you do, but to love who you are.

The Mountain Is You
— by Brianna Wiest

You've climbed over everything life has thrown at you. But now you're the one in your own way. This book is direct, clear, and resonant, written for those who've succeeded by staying focused and detached, but who are now learning to sit with emotion. For Commanders ready to face their own internal resistance, Wiest offers insight without fluff and transformation without collapse.

THE RESCUER (PLAF)

When Helping Hurts: Compassion Fatigue
— by Charles R. Figley

You step in. You soothe. You fix. And you rarely stop to ask what it's costing you. This book gives language to the weariness you may have, normalized compassion fatigue, emotional overload, and burnout from caring too hard for too long. For Rescuers who feel responsible for everyone else's pain, it's a chance to step back without abandoning your care.

The Body is Not an Apology
— by Sonya Renee Taylor

You move through the world offering healing to others. But do you believe your own body, your own story, deserves that same grace? This book is a powerful reclamation for

Rescuers who've spent their lives tending to others while disconnecting from themselves. It's not just about body image, it's about radical self-belonging, the kind you've offered everyone but yourself.

The Language of Letting Go
— by Melody Beattie

You've spent your life trying to ease others' pain. But what do you say to yourself when you're the one unraveling? This daily reader from the author of *Codependent No More* is made for you, with bite-sized reflections to gently challenge guilt, codependency, and emotional overwork. For Rescuers, it's like a quiet check-in from someone who sees your heart and reminds you: it's okay to rest.

Loving What Is
— by Byron Katie

You fix. You soothe. You anticipate. But what if the only thing that needs shifting is the story in your own mind? This book introduces a process called *The Work*, four simple questions that challenge the Rescuer's instinct to take responsibility for everything. With radical honesty and unexpected peace, Katie invites you to find clarity not through control, but through inquiry.

Therapy Isn't Just for White People
— by Kiara Imani

Rescuers often show up for everyone else, especially across cultural and family systems that normalize caretaking. This memoir-meets-guide offers culturally grounded healing for Black readers and anyone navigating inherited burdens. For Rescuers of color, it's both a mirror and a map: your healing matters just as much as your help.

THE WARDEN (PLAS)

Attached
— by Amir Levine and Rachel S. F. Heller

You keep your distance, even when you care deeply. You protect through withdrawal, scanning for danger in closeness. This book helps decode the push-pull of attachment that Warden types often live inside, offering clear insights into why intimacy can feel both magnetic and threatening, and how to begin moving toward connection without losing your sense of control.

Wherever You Go, There You Are
— by Jon Kabat-Zinn

Stillness doesn't come easily when your nervous system is always scanning. But presence doesn't mean exposure; it means choosing to stay with yourself. This book offers Warden types a quiet, spacious invitation into mindfulness not as a performance, but as a practice of softening vigilance and learning how to rest inside your own life.

The Mountain Is You
— by Brianna Wiest

You've built strength by staying self-reliant. But what happens when that mountain you built becomes the thing blocking your view? This book is for Warden types who feel stuck behind their own emotional strategies. Wiest speaks in clear, reflective language, meeting your logic while gently inviting you into feeling. Not to dismantle your defenses, but to understand why they were built and what you want now.

No Bad Parts
— by Dr. Richard Schwartz

You manage chaos by staying composed. But deep inside, there are parts of you still holding fear, hope, and need. This introduction to Internal Family Systems speaks directly to the Warden's instinct to exile emotion. With compassion and clarity, it teaches how to dialogue with your inner protectors, not to eliminate them, but to lead them with care and understanding.

Set Boundaries, Find Peace
— by Nedra Glover Tawwab

You already have boundaries and walls built for safety. But what if boundaries could be bridges instead? This book reframes boundary work not as shutting people out, but as a way to create clarity and connection. For Warden types, it's a practical, no-fluff invitation to stop managing others silently and start communicating from self-trust.

THE DIRECTOR (PDCS)

The Wisdom of Insecurity
— by Alan Watts

You're calm under pressure, composed in crisis, but underneath, certainty is your safety net. This book meets that need for control with something deeper: presence. For Directors who manage life through precision and preparedness, Watts offers a provocative, philosophical shift, one that invites you to find stability not in control, but in surrendering to what is.

Burnout
— by Emily and Amelia Nagoski

You push through. You show up. You hold it down, and you rarely let anyone see the toll it takes. This book is both scientific and affirming, providing Directors with the practical tools to complete the stress cycle and prevent the quiet collapse that comes from overfunctioning. You don't have to earn your rest. You just have to recognize when you've earned your way into exhaustion.

Emotional Agility
— by Susan David

You don't avoid emotion, you manage it with skill. But sometimes, that skill becomes armor. This book speaks directly to Directors who value logic and structure, offering a grounded framework for moving through discomfort with clarity and self-trust. Susan David doesn't ask you to give up control; she teaches you how to steer with more flexibility.

Try Softer
— by Aundi Kolber

You've built your life around trying hard, staying ahead, holding it together, and showing up no matter what. But trying softer isn't a weakness. It's nervous system wisdom. For Directors, this book offers a trauma-informed path to self-compassion, regulation, and rest without losing your edge.

The Perfectionist's Guide to Losing Control
— by Katherine Morgan Schafler

You've turned perfection into purpose, and it's served you well. Until it didn't. This book isn't about dismantling your strengths. It's about reclaiming the parts of you buried beneath pressure. For Directors, it's a validating, high-achiever-centered approach to healing, one that meets your intensity without pathologizing it.

THE HARBOR (PDAS)

Hold Me Tight
— by Dr. Sue Johnson

You show love through steadiness. You stay when others would leave. However, a deep connection requires more than presence; it also demands vulnerability. This book gently guides Harbors into the kind of closeness that doesn't erase you. Built around emotionally focused therapy, it offers a framework for a safe, secure connection where your needs matter just as much as your reliability.

Quiet Power
— by Susan Cain

You're calm. Observant. Thoughtful. And often underestimated. This book doesn't just validate your quiet, it celebrates it. For Harbors who've built strength in stillness, *Quiet Power* reframes that inner world as your greatest asset, while giving you the language to advocate for yourself without having to become loud to be heard.

The Language of Emotions
— by Karla McLaren

You've spent your life regulating the emotional temperature in the room. This book gives you the vocabulary and the validation you've been missing. With compassion and deep insight, McLaren invites Harbors to stop translating everyone else's emotions and start listening to their own. It's not about losing your stillness. It's about giving it a voice.

The Power of Now
— by Eckhart Tolle

You've learned to survive in stillness, but sometimes that stillness hides disconnection. This book offers Harbors a way back into presence without urgency. Tolle's quiet, expansive tone speaks to your love of quiet and helps you recognize how often your calm has been about fear, not peace. With no demands, it invites you back into the moment, gently.

Anxiously Attached
— by Jessica Baum

You want connection but not at the cost of yourself. This book speaks to Harbors who've managed closeness by downplaying their needs. It helps you untangle your desire for intimacy from your habit of disappearing. With a blend of neuroscience, personal story, and attachment theory, Baum offers a healing roadmap that honors your loyalty while helping you show up more fully for yourself and others.